FIRST ISAIAH AND THE DISAPPEARANCE
OF THE GODS

CRITICAL STUDIES IN THE HEBREW BIBLE

Editors
Anselm C. Hagedorn, *University of Osnabrück*
Nathan Macdonald, *University of Cambridge*
Stuart Weeks, *Durham University*

1. *A More Perfect Torah: At the Intersection of Philology and Hermeneutics in Deuteronomy and the Temple Scroll*, by Bernard M. Levinson
2. *The Prophets of Israel*, by Reinhard G. Kratz
3. *Interpreting Ecclesiastes: Readers Old and New*, by Katharine J. Dell
4. *Is There Theology in the Hebrew Bible?* by Konrad Schmid
5. *No Stone Unturned: Greek Inscriptions and Septuagint Vocabulary*, by James K. Aitken
6. *Joel: Scope, Genre(s), and Meaning*, by Ronald L. Troxel
7. *Job's Journey*, by Manfred Oeming and Konrad Schmid
8. *Infant Weeping in Akkadian, Hebrew, and Greek Literature*, by David A. Bosworth
9. *The Development of God in the Old Testament: Three Case Studies in Biblical Theology*, by Markus Witte
10. *"Like a Lone Bird on a Roof": Animal Imagery and the Structure of Psalms*, by Tova L. Forti
11. *A Concise History of Ancient Israel: From the Beginnings Through the Hellenistic Era*, by Bernd U. Schipper
12. *First Isaiah and the Disappearance of the Gods*, by Matthew J. Lynch

First Isaiah and the Disappearance of the Gods

MATTHEW J. LYNCH

EISENBRAUNS | University Park, Pennsylvania

Library of Congress Cataloging-in-Publication Data

Names: Lynch, Matthew, 1979– author.
Title: First Isaiah and the disappearance of the gods / Matthew J. Lynch.
Other titles: Critical studies in the Hebrew Bible ; 12.
Description: University Park, Pennsylvania : Eisenbrauns, [2021] | Series: Critical studies in the Hebrew Bible ; 12 | Includes bibliographical references and index.
Summary: "Examines the rhetorical strategies behind the monotheizing rhetoric of First Isaiah in the Hebrew Bible"—Provided by publisher.
Identifiers: LCCN 2021008067 | ISBN 9781575068398 (paperback)
Subjects: LCSH: Bible. Isaiah, I–XXXIX—Criticism, interpretation, etc. | Rhetoric in the Bible. | Monotheism.
Classification: LCC BS1515.52 .L96 2021 | DDC 224/.106—dc23
LC record available at https://lccn.loc.gov/2021008067

Copyright © 2021 The Pennsylvania State University
All rights reserved
Printed in the United States of America
Published by The Pennsylvania State University Press,
University Park, PA 16802–1003

Eisenbrauns is an imprint of The Pennsylvania State University Press.

The Pennsylvania State University Press is a member of the Association of University Presses.

It is the policy of The Pennsylvania State University Press to use acid-free paper. Publications on uncoated stock satisfy the minimum requirements of American National Standard for Information Sciences—Permanence of Paper for Printed Library Material, ANSI Z39.48–1992.

for Abi

CONTENTS

Abbreviations ix
Acknowledgments xi
Preface xiii

Introduction 1

CHAPTER 1. Rhetoric of Exaltation and Abasement in First Isaiah 19

CHAPTER 2. Yahweh's Exaltation in Isaiah 2:6–22 35

CHAPTER 3. Enemy Boasts and Prophetic Response in Isaiah 10 61

CHAPTER 4. The Folly of the Gods in Isaiah 19 76

CHAPTER 5. Conclusions and Comparison 98

Appendixes 107
Bibliography 111
Index of Subjects 121
Index of Authors 123
Index of Scripture 125

ABBREVIATIONS

ABD *The Anchor Bible Dictionary*, edited by D. N. Freedman. 6 vols. Garden City, NY: Doubleday, 1992
CAD *The Assyrian Dictionary of the Oriental Institute of the University of Chicago*, edited by A. Leo Oppenheim, Erica Reiner, and Martha T. Roth. 21 vols. Chicago: Oriental Institute of the University of Chicago, 1956–2010
CEB Common English Bible
EncJud *Encyclopedia Judaica*, edited by F. Skolnikand M. Berenbaum. 2nd ed. 22 vols. Detroit: Macmillan Reference, 2007
FAT Forschungen zum Alten Testament
HALOT *The Hebrew and Aramaic Lexicon of the Old Testament*, edited by L. Koehler, W. Baumgartner, and J. J. Stamm. Translated and edited under supervision of M. E. J. Richardson. 5 vols. Leiden: Brill, 1994–2000
RIMA Royal Inscriptions of Mesopotamia, Assyrian Periods
RINAP Royal Inscriptions of the Neo-Assyrian Period

ACKNOWLEDGMENTS

This book is the result of work begun during my time with the Sofja Kovalevskaja "Early Jewish Monotheisms" research team at the University of Göttingen. Special thanks to Nathan MacDonald for his leadership of that team. Thanks also to Nathan and the other editors of this Critical Studies in the Hebrew Bible series. Thanks as well to Jim Eisenbraun for accepting this work into the CSHB series. I have benefitted enormously from the feedback and input of several readers, including Hugh Williamson, Chris Hays, Gordon McConville, and Anselm Hagedorn, as well as conversations with Dru Johnson and Brent Strawn. I am also grateful for the research and study time afforded me by Westminster Theological Centre, UK. Thanks to Lucy Peppiatt and the rest of the team there. Finally, I am grateful to Abi for creating an environment that fosters creative thinking and joy.

PREFACE

This book began with an observation that Isa 1–39 uses the unique term אלילים (usually translated "idols") more than anywhere else in the Hebrew Bible. In fact, of its eighteen biblical occurrences, ten of them are in Isa 1–39, suggesting that it might even be a First Isaian neologism. This observation led me on a search to determine the importance of this term within the larger literary and theological landscapes of First Isaiah. What I found bears significance for a theological assessment of First Isaian "monotheism," if this is the right term. Isaiah 1–39 exhibits two rhetorical tendencies that coalesce prominently in the book's second chapter but also ripple throughout First Isaiah in ways that are distinctive from the rest of the book. First, and with a few debated exceptions, First Isaiah steers clear of gracing other deities (and idols) with the status אלהים. Second, First Isaiah makes heavy use of spatial metaphors to emphasize YHWH's "high," "lofty," and "exalted" status in opposition to all that exalted itself. Loftiness and abasement are the terms by which First Isaiah conceptualizes YHWH's categorical supremacy. All other claimants to the heavenly realms were abased before the exalted divine king. In short, First Isaiah displays a unique mode of monotheizing.

Proto-Isaiah's monotheizing rhetoric raises questions in three areas. First, standard accounts of Israelite religion frequently insist that monotheism reached its apex during the exile, especially in Deutero-Isaiah. If this is so, is First Isaiah less monotheistic? And in what sense are we to understand Deutero-Isaiah's monotheizing vis-à-vis First Isaiah? Some scholars at least recognize that Deutero-Isaiah's unique move is not necessarily religious—insofar as it might represent a new stage in Israelite thinking about YHWH's uniqueness—but is instead rhetorical. It represents a rhetorical moment that differs from what preceded. The situation is no different in First Isaiah. I argue that Proto-Isaiah's rhetoric is no less compromising than its Deutero-Isaian counterpart in its insistence that YHWH is categorically supreme, even though First Isaiah's world is different. While I am certainly not the first to insist on First Isaian monotheism, my study focuses on several of the unique rhetorical dimensions of the prophet's monotheizing. It also provides a way of conceptualizing First Isaiah's difference without falling back on worn-out claims about "practical/ethical," as opposed to "pure," monotheism. My observations lend support to studies on the ways First Isaiah makes monotheistic claims about YHWH in the face of Assyrian world-encompassing claims.

Second, as though uncertain that Proto-Isaiah's formulations should stand on their own, some suggest that influence from Deutero-Isaiah or Deuteronomists explains First Isaiah's monotheistic claims. This view assumes that Deutero-Isaiah and Deuteronomistic literature are "known" monotheistic sources that influence otherwise non-monotheistic sources such as First Isaiah. According to this line of thinking, Proto-Isaian critiques of idols and claims about YHWH's supremacy can be explained in terms of literary influences from other monotheistic sources in the Bible. I argue that they cannot, and that First Isaiah portrays YHWH's supremacy in unique terms that deserve their own attention and analysis.

Third, some might question the coherence of Proto-Isaiah's monotheizing. If, for instance, references to the אלילים are redactional, are they in any way part of a coherent monotheizing tendency in this first portion of Isaiah? I argue that, while not every reference to the אלילים coincides with deliberate claims to divine supremacy, Isa 2 links the two explicitly. In so doing, it shapes the reader's perception of YHWH's categorical supremacy. This claim results in an intentional disavowal of all opposing powers.

I will take up these issues in the latter part of the book. My basic claim is that First Isaiah offers a persistent emphasis on YHWH's categorical supremacy alongside a refusal to even grant the idols of Israel and the nations the category "gods."

Introduction

BIBLICAL SCHOLARS ROUTINELY PORTRAY ISA 1–39 as a way station toward the "fully fledged" or "uncompromising" monotheism in Isa 40–55. Because Deutero-Isaiah explicitly denies the existence of other gods, its rhetoric functions as a yardstick for evaluating the rigor and maturity of monotheism in Isaiah's earlier chapters, and for many, the entire Hebrew Bible. In his *Anchor Bible Dictionary* entry on "God," John Scullion remarks that "it is Deutero-Isaiah who expresses most clearly that Israel's God is one and unique, in short, monotheism in its strictest sense."[1] This work suggests that this thinking is wrongheaded. It fails to address the diversity with which biblical writers express YHWH's sole divinity. It ignores the distinctive form that monotheistic rhetoric took in First Isaiah in an effort to assign each monotheistic or quasi-monotheistic text a place in the development of Israelite religion. Tracing monotheism's development is often like trying to trace the development of Israelite beliefs about the inclusion of foreigners, or about any other subject about which the Hebrew Bible speak at various times and in various ways. While development of monotheistic beliefs undoubtedly occurred, I doubt our ability to plot a clear pathway where all arrows point toward an inevitable or climactic Deutero-Isaian-like formulation ("I am, and there is no other"). By contrast, this book proposes that Isa 1–39[2]—itself a complex literary whole—deploys monotheistic rhetoric with no less rigor than Deutero-Isaiah, but that it does so in different ways. While some studies have called attention to the imperial nature of First Isaian monotheism, there are two underexamined aspects to that monotheizing that require further attention. First, Isa 1–39 avoids calling other gods "gods" and instead mocks the very presumption of divinity ascribed to idols. Second, Isa 1–39 deploys some of the Old Testament's most striking spatial language to emphasize YHWH's categorical exaltation and the abasement of all else. In this book, I examine ways that First Isaiah dismisses the gods of the nations through mocking dysphemisms and simultaneously exalts YHWH in uncompromising terms. By refusing to dignify the gods with the term אלהים, they "disappear" from First Isaiah's rhetorical world while only YHWH is supremely exalted. Through a literary and rhetorical analysis of passages using the term אלילים, I suggest that Isa 1–39 offers a powerful assertion of YHWH's sole divinity and supremacy in a world

---

1. Scullion, "God," noted in Kutsko, *Between Heaven and Earth*, 37.
2. I address chs. 36–39 in the book, but not as representative of the monotheizing tendencies found in the poetry of chs. 1–35.

of political counterclaims. We may situate First Isaiah, then, as *a variety* of monotheizing rhetoric that appears in the Hebrew Bible.

This study is not an apologetic for early monotheism. I agree with Hugh Williamson that the texts in which First Isaiah mocks the so-called אלהים as אלילים are quite possibly later redactions (though from when, we cannot be certain). Instead, it is a plea for humility when telling monotheism's story in ancient Israel. We know so little about when Israel first expressed the idea that YHWH belongs in a category of his own, and we know so little about how widespread such beliefs were when they were expressed. We also know even less about how the Hebrew Bible's wide-ranging modes of monotheizing relate to one another.[3] In other words, even a relative chronology of monotheizing texts is difficult. This book looks instead at the monotheizing rhetoric of First Isaiah as one variety of many that take shape across the Hebrew Bible and beyond. Disentangling First Isaiah from a narrative about evolving religious belief helps us hear this remarkable portion of Isaiah on its own terms and then gives us a place from which to reengage with questions about the relationship between this text and others.

Monotheism and the Eighth-Century Prophets

I begin with a look at ways that scholars have assessed monotheism (or not) in First Isaiah. Because many assumed that the whole, or most, of First Isaiah originated in the eighth century BCE, I will address studies that situate First Isaiah in that historical context without committing to that temporal context for the whole of chs. 1–39. My own position is that First Isaiah is a complex literary unity with a long and complex redactional history, much of which we can no longer recover. Nevertheless, much of the scholarship on First Isaiah treats it as a product of the Assyrian period, a point to which I will later return.

Because of developmentalist conceptions of monotheism, Isa 1–39 existed for a long time as a kind of liminal book for scholars of Israelite religion. The prophet was a free bird, beholden neither to the "ritualistic" traditions of the past nor to the more abstract and absolutizing formulations of monotheism that came after him. Instead, with the other eighth-century prophets, he was considered a dynamic soul who led Israel toward the ethical realization that YHWH stood above and beyond Israel. His *ways* were higher, hence his ethical demands on Israel and the nations, and his *domain* was wider, hence his rule over the nations. To take one example from the early part of the last century, George A. Barton argued that First Isaiah followed the prophet Amos's "abhorrence" for ritual,

---

3. See Lynch, "Mapping Monotheism."

and in keeping with monotheistic ideals, envisioned a "higher religious life," even if he consistently "lapsed" back into ritualism.[4] For Barton, the evolution of Israelite religion consisted of a struggle between the higher ethical ideals of Yahwism and the ritualistic tendencies of religion. The four eighth-century prophets embodied a "practical monotheism" that avoided the speculation of later prophets. They simply avoided mention of other deities and proclaimed that YHWH ruled the nations. It was also practical in the sense that it resulted in social and ethical concerns for the poor and needy.[5]

Barton's contemporary George Gray stated with similar conviction that First Isaiah embodied a belief in "virtual monotheism" (anticipated already in Amos), in contrast to the abstract speculative monotheism that followed him. He writes this of Isa 6:

> Neither here nor elsewhere does [First] Isaiah take occasion to assert with precision, like the later Jewish prophet (45:5, 18, 22), that there is no God but Yahweh . . . yet his conception of Yahweh leaves no room for any other being in the same class. . . . The world that is full of Yahweh's glory has no room left in which to reflect the glory of any other God; and if Assyria is Yahweh's instrument (10:5ff.), made merely to serve His purpose . . ., there is no place for any gods of Assyria to control and guide that nation.[6]

Writing later, von Rad suggested that, while the seeds of monotheism's full development are present in Israel's earlier literature, "explicit monotheism" does not develop until Second Isaiah. Monotheism only emerged through confrontation with the gods of Canaan, the Assyrian threat, and eventually, in exile. Von Rad argued that, unlike traditional cultic proponents in Israel, the prophets "are much freer from traditional formulations."[7] What they say, he argues, is much closer to their own beliefs and ideas, for they stood on their own.[8] Faced with the Assyrian threat, prophets such as First Isaiah and Amos asked, who was really lord in the sphere of history? "The lordly silence with which Isaiah or Amos pass over the gods of the nations," he remarks, "is of real significance." Von Rad may be alluding to First Isaiah's silence about gods in the oracles against the nations (chs. 13–23). That silence is pregnant. Isaiah "leaves no place

---

4. Barton, *Religion of Israel*, 161.
5. Ibid., 94–97.
6. Gray, *Book of Isaiah, I–XXVII*, lxxxvi. He suggests that "there may be room to question the absoluteness, and certainly the explicitness, of the monotheism of the prophets of the 8th century; [but] there can be no doubt of the intensity with which they apprehended Yahweh as a distinct and living personality" (p. lxxxvii).
7. Von Rad, *Old Testament Theology*, 1:212.
8. Ibid., 2:177. For a critique of the image of a lone prophet, see Wilson, *Prophecy and Society in Ancient Israel*.

whatsoever for the gods of other nations or any functions they might exercise."[9] This prepares the ground for Deutero-Isaiah, a prophet who with "conscious ... theological reflexion" offers a clear monotheistic expression: "I am Jahweh, besides me there is no God."[10]

Von Rad argues similarly in his later published *God at Work in Israel*. There, he argues that YHWH's world-encompassing power rebalanced the prevailing assumption that Assyria stood atop the imperial heap. Assyria was a mere tool in God's hands. Noting again the absence of Assyrian gods in First Isaiah, he emphasizes how God's plans alone drive history. For von Rad, this view of history leaves no room for the nations' gods. "They are deprived of power," he writes, and so much so that when speaking about God's visitation, First Isaiah "can speak only with grim humor about the fate of idols and idols worshipers" (p. 136). For von Rad, this is monotheism, and "much more than monotheism; in Isaiah we meet an ultimate comforting message that interprets man's existence in history with reference to God's coming and therewith the removal of power from the idols."[11] His point here, as he later insists with reference to Deutero-Isaiah, is that monotheistic formulations in First Isaiah (and Second) are not abstract philosophical musings. They are borne out of the particular struggle of a politically disadvantaged people and speak into their specific historical hopes.[12]

Not all see the prophet's monotheism in such terms. Many claim that First Isaiah, with other eighth-century prophets, paved the way for monotheism by hastening Israel's break from its national "limitations."[13] Rainer Albertz proposes that the eighth-century prophets prepared Israel for universalized understandings of divinity in the exile. He builds on the early work of scholars such as Wilhelm Vatke (1835), who posited a distinction between early Israelite religion, prophetic religion, and the religion that emerged in the postexilic period. Vatke's "rather bloodless outline" of Israelite religion took further shape under Wellhausen, Keunen, and then Smend. In particular, Smend adopts Vatke's threefold schema but saw the second prophetic stage as the climax of Israel's religious development. The prophetic literature "universalized and individualized the national religion of Israel, separated it from the world, and led it to a higher morality."[14] Albertz critiques Smend's Christianized history, as well as his inattention to social and comparative dimensions of the development of

---

9. Von Rad, *Old Testament Theology*, 1:212.
10. Ibid. Even with Deutero-Isaiah, however, von Rad insists that his confession of monotheism is not a "truth based on a philosophy of religion." Instead, its truth is only made credible through confession and loyalty to YHWH.
11. Von Rad, "Origin of Mosaic Monotheism," 136–37.
12. Ibid., 137.
13. For an important critique of such anti-particularism, see Levenson, "Universal Horizon of Biblical Particularism."
14. Albertz, *History of Israelite Religion*, 1:6.

Israelite religion. Nevertheless, Albertz's fascination with Vatke's and Smend's assessments of the prophetic stage is clear.[15]

For Albertz, the prophets not only extend the idea of divine power beyond previous national and religious confines. They also uncouple such ideas from any accompanying extension of *Israel's* power. "The power of God," he writes, "becomes a critical, destabilizing element which puts the existence of their own state in question." Albertz presses the point in terms of an in-principle objection to the nationalism and parochialism of the temple and cult. The prophets thus undertake "manifold distancings" of YHWH from the state. YHWH transcends the economic order, the monarchy, political and military power, and "even his own cult."[16] The prophets, along with their disciples, model a kind of personal piety that then "became the most important vehicle for official Yahweh religion in the exile, after the institutions of the state and cult collapsed in 587."[17] Albertz's formulation reflects the ideal of "ethical monotheism" that finds its origins in Keunen and Wellhausen. As a God who was "other," Israel's deity was able to stand over against the nation in judgment and to uphold an ethical order that was universal.[18]

More recently, Mark Smith has connected the emergence of monotheism to the collapse Israelite society.[19] The destruction of Judah's countryside by Sennacherib in 701 BCE alongside the aniconic reforms of Hezekiah and Josiah led to concomitant breakdowns in traditional family structures. These breakdowns, Smith argues, led Israel to theorize parallel breakdowns in the divine realm: "A culture with a diminished lineage system, one less embedded in traditional family patrimonies due to societal changes in the eighth through sixth centuries, might be more predisposed both to hold to individual human accountability for behavior and to see an individual deity accountable for the cosmos. … Accordingly, later Israelite monotheism was denuded of the divine family, perhaps reflecting Israel's weakening family lineages and patrimonies."[20] Smith then suggests that "monotheistic claims made sense in a world where political boundaries or institutions no longer offered any middle ground."[21]

These proposals, in varying ways, posit a teleology according to which monotheism evolved steadily beyond its national confines, with its traditional social and political structures.[22] The prophets allegedly aided that break with the

---

15. It should be noted that Albertz insists that a history of Israelite religion must not adopt the "anti-Judaistic Christian prejudices" of his predecessors (ibid., 1:12).
16. Ibid., 1:176.
17. Ibid., 1:180.
18. MacDonald, *Deuteronomy*, 24–29.
19. Smith builds on the work of Halpern, "Jerusalem and the Lineages."
20. Smith, *Origins of Biblical Monotheism*, 164.
21. Ibid., 195.
22. Lynch, *Monotheism and Institutions*, 9.

past by imagining new relationships between YHWH, the nations, and their gods for late preexilic and exilic contexts. This process had its clearest and natural conclusion and home in Deutero-Isaiah.

The examples above highlight the way scholars have tended to see First Isaiah and the other eighth-century prophets standing at a crossroads in Israelite religion. They were considered the first free thinkers in Israel, able to see beyond the confines of land and nation due to their ethically enlightened beliefs and increasingly sociopolitical homelessness. Moreover, the story of monotheism's assumed a shift from *political* assertions of YHWH's power over the nations (and accompanying ethical superiority) toward a *philosophical* reflection on that extension of power and all it meant for religion. This deeply entrenched pattern feeds a scholarly narrative that First Isaiah's monotheizing was somehow incomplete and also that Second Isaiah's monotheism is abstract and philosophical. Neither does justice to the terms by which each corpus represents YHWH's sole divinity. Scholarship was, and to some extent still is, marked by a striking inattention to the ways that these prophets actually formulate their God claims. Scholars assumed that any move toward the assertion of YHWH's political hegemony over the nations involved a move toward monotheism. Conversely, anything national or parochial was considered to be at odds with YHWH's sole divinity. Furthermore, scholars assumed a link between monotheism and ethics, and thus each instance of concern for the poor became an instance of practical or ethical monotheism. Each eighth-century prophet became an instance of that religio-historical shift—birthed in politics.

Renewed interest in the shape of First Isaiah's theological world coincides with redaction-critical reflection on the nature of First Isaiah. Those who argue for monotheistic beliefs in First Isaiah tend to do so on the assumption that the book derives, *en masse*, from an eighth-century prophet or thereabouts. But if the book is instead the result of a complex redactional process that goes well beyond the eighth century, what can be said of "monotheism in First Isaiah"? The most frequent answer, it seems, is that monotheistic impulses originate in other "known" biblical sources that might have influenced the prophet. The assumption is that Isa 1–35 lacks a distinct or coherent enough monotheism to advance such claims on its own. As we will see in the course of this study, many will attribute any monotheistic language in the book to a Deuteronomistic redactor, or to Second Isaiah. Such attempts to locate monotheistic influences elsewhere miss the distinctiveness with which First Isaian monotheistic rhetoric takes shape. In the chapters that follow, I suggest that even though the book is likely the result of a long and complex redactional process (including by Deutero-Isaiah), we may still speak of First Isaian monotheistic discourse that carries its own unique constellation of features. While possessing clear links to Second Isaiah (and elsewhere), the book nevertheless has its own theological contributions to make.

Such a claim presupposes that we can speak about a body of literature called First Isaiah. For this study, I refer to First Isaiah as the body of literature stretching from Isa 1–35,[23] which was then supplemented canonically with a section of narrative literature (chs. 36–39) as a bridge to what follows in the book. Isaiah 1–35 undoubtedly underwent a complex redaction history. However, chs. 1–35 are unified in large measure by their literary orientation toward the concerns and hopes surrounding Israel's confrontation with the Assyrian Empire. This does not mean that all texts in chs. 1–35 originated in the Assyrian period. Instead, as later texts were added to texts that did originate in the Assyrian period, they conformed to those earlier concerns. The rhetoric of First Isaiah also exhibits such marked differences from the rest of the book that we can speak of a generally differentiated vocabulary (I explore this in appendixes 1 and 2).[24] The focus in my work is to analyze texts employing the term אלילים and spatial metaphors for God to emphasize the unique critique of the "gods" in First Isaiah. This critique (a) differs from critiques in DI or DtrH, or other prophetic books and (b) is literarily dependent on the Assyria-focused prophecies of First Isaiah, even though they may originate from later times. While it may be that many of the אלילים texts are redactional and later (insofar as we can tell), they are nonetheless drawn into a rhetorical world in First Isaiah that is Assyria-facing. I do not mean to imply, however, that the redactional qualities of the אלילים texts are insignificant. They certainly nudge the direction of earlier prophecies toward concerns over false deities. But before doing so, let us take a closer look at the ways that First Isaiah features in discussions about monotheism.

First Isaiah and Monotheism in Recent Scholarship

Recent scholarly conversations on monotheism in First Isaiah have tended to revolve around the impact of, and responses to, the Assyrian crisis in the eighth century. While von Rad and George Gray before him attend to the Assyrian context of First Isaiah's exalted claims about YHWH, it was not until more recently that comparative studies drew clearer attention to the impact of Neo-Assyrian ideology on First Isaiah. It is important to reemphasize that even for those who do not assign all First Isaian texts to the eighth century, the memories of Israel's confrontations with Assyria reverberate across the book. Several recent studies highlight the significant role that Neo-Assyrian rhetoric and ideology played in the formulation of First Isaian monotheism. Baruch Levine's study is an

---

23. One might focus, even more specifically, on chs. 1–33, since chs. 34–35 appear to be almost wholly redactional bridges between First and Second Isaiah. Chapters 24–27 are often recognized to be much later in their entirety, though Christopher B. Hays makes a strong case for the inclusion of great portions of these chapters in the Assyrian period. See his recent book, *Origins of Isaiah 24–27*.

24. On the distinctiveness of First Isaiah's rhetoric, see Couey, *Reading the Poetry*.

example. He writes: "It was the threat to the survival of Judah and Jerusalem, emanating from Assyria, which called forth an enhanced God-idea. That idea evolved into universal monotheism, and in effect, enabled the people of Israel to survive exile and domination by successive world empires. In such terms, universal monotheism is to be seen as a religious response to empire, an enduring world-view founded on the proposition that all power exercised by humans, no matter how grandiose, is transient, and ultimately subservient to a divine plan for the whole earth, for all nations."[25] For Levine, the Assyrian threats of the eighth century led Israel's prophets toward an augmented conception of God's power and universal rule. This augmented conception was every bit as far-reaching as Deutero-Isaiah's. But Deutero-Isaiah's assertions of YHWH's power over the nation would not have been possible without the Assyrian provocation. Evolutionary assumptions are also evident in Levine's argument. Israel shifted from a "national agenda" seen in the conquest-settlement tradition toward an international agenda. While Israel's exodus traditions also exhibit international extensions of divine power, Levine insists that those traditions "belong[s] with the conquest-settlement traditions." For Levine, Israel's prophets participated in that national zeal through increasingly polemical engagements with the gods of Canaan: "The fervor of the national movement led to the progressive paring-away of gods and goddesses, and the exaltation of the national God, Yahweh."[26] But the Assyrian threat also provoked a "crisis of faith," evident in prophecies of Hosea and Amos, such that Israel's henotheistic faith became "untenable." First Isaiah marks the beginning of monotheism by declaring YHWH "sole sovereign over all nations."[27] Levine thus posits a clear movement from the *national* concerns of early Israel toward the *international* concerns of First Isaiah. The "global horizon" of passages such as Isa 10:5–19 leave no doubt in his mind that the prophet believes that YHWH "is the only true God."[28]

Other scholars focus specifically on First Isaiah's imitation of imperialist claims. Peter Machinist details specific idioms and themes that reflect direct and indirect cultural contact.[29] Among the examples Machinist examines, most reflect attempts to apply claims to hegemony and glory—traditionally ascribed to the Assyrian monarch—to YHWH. As Judean ambassadors traveled to Assyrian capitals and as Assyria exerted its influence on Judah, Isaiah found occasion to imitate such imperial rhetoric. For Machinist, First YHWH's control of the

---

25. Levine, "Assyrian Ideology," 411; cf. Levine, "'Ah, Assyria! Rod of My Rage.'"
26. Levine, "Assyrian Ideology," 415.
27. Ibid., 416.
28. Ibid., 422.
29. Machinist, "Assyria and Its Image in First Isaiah"; Machinist, "Once More"; cf. Parpola, "Assyrian Tree of Life"; Schipper, "'City by the Sea'"; Halpern, "'Brisker Pipes Than Poetry.'"

nations reflects a broad process of absorbing "in a henotheistic way" the powers that typically belonged to the Assyrian deities.

Shawn Aster goes further in his study. For Aster, YHWH's claims to power imitate and ultimately subvert claims by the god Assur. Whereas Assur claimed universal sovereignty through his human counterpart, the king, YHWH exercised sovereignty *despite* any human counterpart. The depiction of YHWH was even more transcendent than the Assyrian deity:[30] "The idea of YHWH's transcendence also makes the discussion of monotheism vs. henotheism somewhat redundant. For only if YHWH exists as supreme over time and space and wholly without parallel in the earthly sphere, are any other powers not his equals. Whether such powers are called 'gods' or 'celestial beings' no longer matters, for they exist in the realm of constrained power, whereas YHWH is unconstrained and supreme."[31] The fact that First Isaiah betrays thoroughgoing knowledge of the deity Assur, but never gives him a mention, lends further credence to YHWH's total and uncontested rule. "There is no need for God to battle gods," Aster writes. Instead, the battle takes place in the realm of "imperial ideology." By "refusing to engage in any sort of polemic about Assur, [Isaiah] refused to recognize his existence."[32]

Reflection and Critique

The foregoing historical sketch provokes several observations relating to monotheism and First Isaiah. First, earlier critical biblical scholarship tended to lump First Isaiah in with other eighth-century prophets. Together, they formed a kind of golden age when monotheism was instinctual and less philosophical. It was ethical and dynamic but lacked the sharper articulations that characterized Second Isaiah's uncompromising monotheism. They embodied a kind of free-spirited individualism and ethical awakening that presaged later developments in Christianity. Their ethical monotheism was practical and applied, though not yet philosophically formed.

Second, we observed a scholarly tendency to draw a direct line between the international elements of First Isaiah and the emergence of monotheism. The more dubious versions of this theory insist that the move toward monotheism involved a rejection of "national" or "particularist" concerns. The image of prophets as social revolutionaries may play a role here. The assumption is that insofar as the prophets break with traditions of the past, they simultaneously

---

30. Aster, *Reflections of Empire*, 39.
31. Ibid., 39–40.
32. Ibid., 40, 132, 277.

open new theological possibilities. However, it proves difficult to detect any move "beyond" the land, temple, cult, and kingship in First Isaiah. Even Deutero-Isaiah announces a return to the land and the rebuilding of the temple (Isa 44:24–28; 46:13), and Trito-Isaiah assumes worship at the temple (Isa 56; 60–62; 66). But in addition to the retention of national concerns, scholars typically fail to explain the uniqueness of First Isaiah's supposedly more "international" perspective when compared with other Old Testament texts Exod 15, which seem equally broad in scope. Levine's insistence that the exodus belongs to the conquest-settlement tradition—and therefore does not qualify—fails to address the issue.[33] Tone-deafness to the localized nature of all monotheistic texts seems to parallel scholarly inattention to the possible ways that monotheistic discourse could take shape. This study aims to address this with its study of First Isaiah. Monotheistic rhetoric was not moving toward a uniform end.

Third, the literature of Second Isaiah still seems to play a controlling function. It serves as a standard for measuring the relative purity of the prophet's monotheistic discourse. The Assyrian turn allegedly put Israel on a trajectory from its earlier parochialism to the internationalist perspectives of Deutero-Isaiah. Scholars consistently compare First and Second Isaiah in terms of implicit (or unreflective) monotheism versus explicit (and reflective) monotheism. In these formulations, First Isaiah rendered monotheism inevitable, but did not necessarily aim to assert YHWH's sole divinity. For some, First Isaiah does not fully tip the balance toward monotheism but nonetheless plays a key role in laying the theological foundations for its eventual emergence. With few exceptions, however, scholars agree that First Isaiah leaves very little room for other divine or human sovereigns but YHWH.[34] In this, they echo von Rad's statement that, because of YHWH's "absolute power" over the nations, "there is room for no other actor in history."[35] The regular contrast between First and Second Isaiah assumes that the latter offers a more reflective, or conscious, emphasis on YHWH's sole divinity as such.

Fourth, more-recent comparative studies have set First Isaiah on its own footing vis-à-vis an Assyrian context. They suggest that the Assyrian crisis of the eighth and seventh centuries provided the historical impetus for First Isaiah's monotheizing (or implicit monotheism). Faced with claims about Assyrian hegemony, Isaiah insisted that YHWH controlled the Assyrian Empire and would eventually bring it to judgment. This belief either prepared the way for or rendered certain the concomitant belief that the gods of the great empires were powerless. The shift toward belief in YHWH's sovereignty over the Assyrians

---

33. Levine, "Assyrian Ideology," 415.
34. See Wildberger, *Isaiah 28–39*, 618, as well as his broader discussion on pp. 617–49.
35. Von Rad, *Old Testament Theology*, 2:183.

marks, for many, a key to understanding how monotheism emerged in Israel.³⁶ Nevertheless, such studies are not always careful about how they use the term *monotheism*, applying it, for instance, to explain YHWH's control over the nations. In addition, redaction-critical studies raise questions about the degree to which all the theological claims in chs. 1–39 can be positioned as an Assyrian "response." This said, the attention to the political forces at work in First Isaiah is most welcome. My study of the אלילים and accompanying monotheistic rhetoric provides a way to deepen such analysis by attending to the nuanced ways that YHWH's political supremacy featured in a world shaped by the memory of Israel's encounters with Assyria (and other nations).

Fifth, scholars rarely reflect on the usefulness of using monotheism as an analytical category in First Isaiah. Such lack of reflection seems to stem from the history of religions framework within which the concept of monotheism typically operates. This framework tends to highlight, or at least search for, the key moments when religious ideas emerged or broke through earlier forms. It is far less interested in how and whether the language of "monotheism" helps illuminate the poetics of First Isaiah itself. Moreover, because of monotheism's emphasis on the number of deities in existence, First Isaiah can be something of a nonstarter. It rarely, if ever, mentions the names of foreign or domestic deities other than YHWH.³⁷ Many studies of First Isaiah simply do not mention the subject. I suggest that the question of monotheism helps us understand First Isaiah's rhetoric, but the meaning of monotheism requires clarification. In addition, it proves more useful to take the discussion of First Isaian monotheism out of the realm of evolving religious ideas and to examine it instead as a rhetorical phenomenon in its own right. My point is not that rhetorical assertions are devoid of theological content or bear no relation to developing ideas. However, it is essential to understand the distinctive theological claims of First Isaiah in terms of its own rhetorical aims, including points of continuity and discontinuity with other theological claims, especially in Second Isaiah.

For monotheism to prove useful as an analytical tool, my use of the term requires clarification. I will discuss this below, but I emphasize here that scholars are generally unclear about how they use the term. Von Rad is an exception. He recognizes the limits of the term *monotheism* and resists any attempt to associate its emergence with "a philosophic reduction of the multiplicity of numinous phenomena to the view of them as one."³⁸ He also resists any attempt to join the prophets together as if addressing "a single idea—that of ethical

---

36. Machinist, "Once More," 38.
37. I will discuss possible connections between Enlil and אליל below.
38. Von Rad, *Old Testament Theology*, 1:211. See discussion of von Rad and monotheism in MacDonald, *Deuteronomy*, 40–42.

monotheism."³⁹ Instead, their messages (and accompanying theology) were particular to the circumstances and needs of the moment. To this extent, von Rad anticipates some of the literary and rhetorical approaches to monotheism adopted by later biblical scholars.⁴⁰ In what follows, I outline an approach to monotheism that will set the stage for my study of First Isaiah. I will draw from my previous research on the analytical limits and potential of monotheism as a concept.⁴¹

Defining Monotheism

By way of background, there are good reasons to avoid use of the term *monotheism*. Its origins and development as a concept within the context of seventeenth-century Cambridge Platonism, and then within Enlightenment philosophical thought, raise the specter of anachronism when applied to eighth-century Israelite prophecy. In particular, the term tends to carry a set of corollaries that may be ill-suited to the biblical subject matter or to the particular texts at hand. For instance, some will insist that monotheism necessarily implies an emphasis on YHWH as creator,⁴² hence his transcendent distinctiveness from all reality. For others, it implies a rejection of magic, all other divine beings, or even the cult.⁴³ Still others suggest that monotheism involves belief in the significance of the individual or in a transnational morality. The sheer range of monotheism's entailments bewilders. It seems to provide a handy way to project one's favored beliefs onto the ancients. As MacDonald argues, this tendency was certainly operative from the initial formulation of the concept, and through the Enlightenment as monotheism provided a clear way to distinguish the Christian religion from paganism.⁴⁴

Yet the threat of anachronism, and the ill-conceived uses of a given concept, do not negate its potential usefulness. Such risks beset any attempt to explain the past using nonnative terms. Jonathan Z. Smith observes that a term such as *religion* is not necessarily native to the subject that scholars of religion

---

39. Von Rad, *Old Testament Theology*, 2:188, 298.
40. But on the other hand, von Rad assumes that Deutero-Isaiah's monotheism was, by contrast to the implied monotheism of earlier times, "the conscious product of theological reflexion" (ibid., 211).
41. Lynch, *Monotheism and Institutions*; Lynch, "Mapping Monotheism"; Lynch, "Monotheism in Ancient Israel."
42. This emphasis finds its clearest expression in the work of Kaufmann, *Religion of Israel*, 137. Others followed Kauffmann's lead, including Bauckham, *Jesus and the God of Israel*, 84–85; Sommer, *Bodies of God*, 246–47.
43. See MacDonald's discussion of Keunen in *Deuteronomy*, 38–39.
44. See Assmann, *Moses the Egyptian*, 17–21.

study. Nevertheless, the term can establish a "disciplinary horizon," and as such, "second-order categor[ies]" such as religion can prove productive by their very distance from the subject they study.[45] As a second-order category, monotheism enables interpreters of the Old Testament to ask certain questions of the text that set the terms for its discussion. It also provides a criterion for data selection as we examine the text and then for comparison with other biblical texts deemed monotheistic.[46]

However, the text needs to be given its turn to ask questions of the category itself. That is the function of the distance Smith mentions. We have seen already that First Isaiah plays a role—albeit subservient to Deutero-Isaiah—in the history of biblical scholarship on monotheism. But this has often been done unreflectively, as if the meaning and relevance of monotheism for Isa 1–39 were obvious. But we are better served by exploring the degree to which First Isaiah adapts or resists the categorization itself or perhaps calls for an inflation or modification of the term's meaning.[47] Moreover, once the category "monotheism" has done its heuristic work of organizing the data for selection, the category itself, to some extent, recedes into the background.[48] The usefulness of any heuristic category is the degree to which it enables interpreters to make meaningful claims about the text, and comparisons to other texts ostensibly within the same category.[49]

I suggest that speaking about *monotheistic rhetoric* is a more useful category than monotheism, when speaking of the kind of claims First Isaiah makes. Here is a case for the importance of this category that I made elsewhere:

> My decision to focus on rhetoric derives from a desire to avoid speculation about the theological assumptions of biblical writers, focusing instead on the theological import of their rhetorical claims. I am interested in how monotheistic rhetoric works in context (as a proximate goal), and what it accomplishes theologically (as an ultimate goal), but not in the underlying beliefs of writers. Texts employing monotheistic rhetoric do not always paint a sufficiently broad picture for one to determine with certainty that a writer's beliefs were consistently monotheistic, just as one could not derive a monotheistic belief system on the basis of expressions in certain Akkadian and Egyptian hymns that espouse the sole divinity of a given deity. Authors do not always reveal their theological presuppositions; neither do they always hold them consistently. They can, however,

---

45. Smith, *Relating Religion*, 193–94 and 207–8; cited in Smith, "Monotheism," 280.
46. Satlow, "Disappearing Categories," 293.
47. On the inflation of terms, see Dwyer, "Violence and Its Histories."
48. Satlow, "Disappearing Categories," 294.
49. Ibid., 295.

deploy rhetoric that distinguishes YHWH in absolute terms, even if only for a rhetorical moment.[50]

Several studies in the past two decades have attended to the rhetorical dimensions of monotheistic claims in the Hebrew Bible. In his book *The Origins of Biblical Monotheism*, Smith observes that claims about YHWH's sole divinity are "rhetorical, designed as much to persuade and reinforce as it is to assert."[51] For Smith, the presence of monotheistic rhetoric does not necessarily indicate the presence of a "monotheistic culture" or underlying monotheistic belief system. Instead, it "explain[ed] Yahwistic monolatry in absolute terms. Monotheism reinforced Israel's exclusive relationship with its deity."[52] Of course, this presupposes clarity on what monotheism *is* in each context. Given that the term itself does not appear in the Hebrew Bible, one has to establish a horizon of inquiry toward which a study of monotheistic rhetoric might orient itself. As Walter Moberly notes, it is critical to find out "what is, and is not, meant by [YHWH's oneness] in its various contexts."[53] Attending to monotheism as a mode of persuasion complicates attempts to arrange the text into "neat historical phases," but simultaneously clarifies the purposes toward which biblical writers struggled to affirm YHWH's exclusive prerogatives and supremacy.[54]

With these sensitivities in view, I propose a heuristic description of monotheistic rhetoric that allows for a wider possible range of monotheistic configurations in the Hebrew Bible, that avoids the chronological preoccupations of the *Religionsgeschichtliche Schule*, and that resists abstractions that run rough-shod over the actual contexts in which claims about divinity are embedded. Quoting from my earlier article: "Monotheistic rhetoric, I suggest, entails *the expression of* YHWH*'s categorical supremacy, or supreme uniqueness*. That is, monotheism involves locating YHWH in a class of his own that is uniquely distinguished from all other reality, or at least the realities deemed threatening to YHWH's utter distinctiveness. Phrased as a question, one might ask, *What are the ways that a given text forges divisions between* YHWH *and all else such that he is 'one/alone'?*"[55] This definition allows us to ask, what are the terms by which the writers of First Isaiah distinguish YHWH in absolute terms? What are the ways that those constructions of YHWH's supremacy are similar to, or different from, the constructions of YHWH's status in Isa 40–55 or other bodies of literature?

---

50. Lynch, "Mapping Monotheism," 49.
51. Smith, *Origins of Biblical Monotheism*, 153.
52. Ibid., 154.
53. Moberly, "How Appropriate Is 'Monotheism?'" 233.
54. Hays, "Religio-Historical Approaches," 180.
55. Lynch, "Mapping Monotheism," 50.

Monotheizing by Omission and Exaltation

In his 2000 publication *Between Heaven and Earth: Divine Presence and Absence in the Book of Ezekiel*, John Kutsko critiqued the presumption that Deutero-Isaiah was the Hebrew Bible's strongest proponent of monotheism.[56] While Deutero-Isaiah affirms YHWH's sole divinity through image-maker polemics, and through "sole existence" clauses (e.g., אין עוד), Ezekiel "appears to struggle with the very use of the term *ʾĕlōhîm*."[57] Thus, Ezekiel never uses אלהים in reference to idols or pagan deities, but rather, he employs a diverse vocabulary of substitute terms that deride idols' presumption to divinity (e.g., גלולים).[58] Moreover, Ezekiel modifies Deuteronomic phrases that refer to other deities (e.g., זנה/הלך אחרי אלהים) in favor of those that lack אלהים (e.g., זנה/הלך/תעה אחרי גלולים).[59] Kutsko states: "This aversion, this avoidance of any association that might legitimize a god other than Yahweh has far-reaching implications, for it suggests that Ezekiel was clearly monotheistic, accomplishing his goal in ways different from Deutero-Isaiah but consciously carrying his conviction to a radical extreme in his terminology. Unlike Deutero-Isaiah, the prophet Ezekiel is rarely invoked as a theological voice contributing to the development of monotheism in the religion of Israel. Quite the opposite is true, however; he is one of its loudest voices."[60] Sven Petry and others have made similar observations regarding Ezekiel's monotheistic rhetoric and its use of substituted derisive terms for אלהים.[61] And despite such recognition that Ezekiel, Priestly, and other Priestly-inspired literature engages in a different form of monotheistic rhetoric, it is surprising that an analogous phenomenon in First Isaiah has received such little attention, with the exception of Hugh Williamson's article on the אלילים

---

56. Kutsko, *Between Heaven and Earth*, 38.
57. Ibid.
58. The question as to whether these critique idols has now been raised by Margaret Odell, in her forthcoming article, "Did Ezekiel Condemn Idolatry? A Re-examination of the Nature and Function of the גלולים in the Book of Ezekiel," *JBL* (forthcoming). I thank Margaret for an advanced copy of this article.
59. Kutsko, *Between Heaven and Earth*, 39. Interestingly, Kutsko notes how the Targumim (*Tg. Neof.*, *Tg. Onq.*, *Tg. Ps.-J.*) follow Ezekiel's lead by systematically substituting the Aramaic טעות ("idols") for אלהים. Similarly, Kutsko notes that Ezekiel transforms the Deuteronomic phrase עבד אלהים . . . עץ ואבן, "to serve gods . . . of wood and stone" (Deut 4:28; 28:36; 28:64) with שרת עץ ואבן, "to worship wood and stone" (Ezek 20:32; p. 39).
60. Ibid., 41–42.
61. Petry, *Die Entgrenzung JHWHS*, 377–78.

in Isaiah.⁶² In the unique material of First Isaiah, encompassing parts of Isaiah 1–35, the prophet nearly always avoids use of the term אלהים in reference to any but YHWH, preferring instead the dysphemistic term אלילים, which seems to be a mocking distortion of the term אלהים.⁶³ Of its eighteen biblical occurrences, אלילים occurs ten times in First Isaiah,⁶⁴ and then nowhere else in the book.

At the same time, Isa 1–39 asserts YHWH's supremacy with remarkable force. Several scholars mentioned already suggest that Israel's political contact with Assyrian claims to hegemony explain this phenomenon. My study supports such studies without pinning down chs. 1–39 in the Neo-Assyrian period. Moreover, it supplements studies of Neo-Assyrian reflexes in Isaiah by attending specifically to the nature and function of absolutizing rhetoric in the book. This absolutizing occurs in two significant ways. First, Isa 1–39 emphasizes YHWH's supreme exaltation in spatial terms. Isaiah 6 has received the most attention in this regard. But the emphasis on YHWH's exalted status continues, most notably in the book's early chapters. Proto-Isaiah draws the reader's attention to YHWH's elevated status by frontloading assertions to this effect toward the beginning of the book. In Isa 2 the prophet deploys the verbs *נשא ("to lift," 6×), *רום ("to be lofty," 5×), *שגב ("to be exalted," 2×) more than anywhere else in the book. While asserting YHWH's loftiness, the prophet also claims YHWH's opposition to all that is high and lifted. Other sections of First Isaiah use language similar to Isa 2 to assert YHWH's exaltation and the abasement of all else (e.g., 5:15–16; 33:5, 10). The claim here is not that Second Isaiah lacks a similar insistence on YHWH's supremacy but instead that First Isaiah uses unique spatial metaphors that lack equivalents in the rest of Isaiah.

Second, Isa 1–39 uses unique names for YHWH, which seem to emphasize his exclusive political and military sovereignty. These include האדון ("the sovereign one"), יהוה צבאות ("YHWH of hosts"),⁶⁵ and other names. These names reflect efforts to absolutize divine power and authority vis-à-vis political claims to the contrary.

As I suggest throughout this book, the use of אלילים along with these two features contribute to Isa 1–39's broader effort to distinguish YHWH in absolute terms. To these features I would also hasten to add that First Isaiah reflects

---

62. Williamson, "Idols in Isaiah."
63. I will return to the question of the relationship between Isa 1–35 and chs. 36–39 below. Most scholars believe Isa 36–39 derive from 2 Kgs 18–20, with some notable passages that seem to derive from Isaiah (e.g., Isa 37:22–29; 38:9–20). Though there remains debate concerning the precise relationship between Isa 36–39 and 2 Kgs 18–20, the monotheistic claims in Isa 37:16–20 (/// 2 Kgs 19:15–19) are in clear continuity with similar language in the Deuteronomistic History (e.g., 1 Kgs 8), and lack any parallel in Isa 1–35.
64. Isa 2:8, 18, 20 (2×); 10:10 (sg.), 11; 19:1, 3; 31:7 (2×).
65. האדון appears in 5 of 6 biblical occurrences: Isa 1:24; 3:1; 10:16, 33; 19:4; cf. Mal 3:1. יהוה צבאות appears 53× vs. 7× in the rest of the book.

imitation of absolutizing claims to power evident in Assyrian rhetoric.[66] Like Ezekiel, First Isaiah is hardly more compromising and absolute than Deutero-Isaiah in its rhetoric of divine supremacy. Deutero-Isaiah marks a rhetorical shift in language about YHWH but not a heightening or deepening of YHWH's categorical supremacy.

However, to sustain this argument, it will be important (a) to explain the terms in which YHWH's categorical uniqueness takes shape in First Isaiah and (b) to demonstrate that First Isaiah has a unique theological voice—that its claims about divine supremacy are not simply Deutero-Isaian or Deuteronomistic in origin, as several scholars claim. Regarding (a) above, I agree with others such as Baruch Levine, Shawn Aster, Peter Machinist, and others that First Isaiah expresses YHWH's categorical uniqueness in decidedly political terms. Isaiah is insistent that YHWH is sole sovereign, and that foreign alliances were a direct affront to YHWH's claims. My study supplements their studies by analyzing the pervasive rhetoric of exaltation and abasement by which First Isaiah expresses those political claims. First Isaiah begins with a tirade against all that is "raised up" (Isa 2) and concludes with the dramatic defeat of King Sennacherib for his boasts (Isa 36–39). While this study does not outline the entirety of that political theology, my discussion of divine supremacy makes best sense against the backdrop of rival imperial claims.

Regarding (b), I will show in this book how First Isaiah develops its own ways of asserting YHWH's sole divinity that are not demonstrably influenced by Second Isaiah and are not simply explainable as Deuteronomistic interpolations (as sometimes suggested). I suggest that one cannot simply attribute First Isaiah's monotheizing moves to other, monotheistic, redactors of chs. 1–35. Yet, the study resists an easy attribution of monotheism to the Neo-Assyrian period, at least in its final form. It is rather the Neo-Assyrian *legacy* that echoes through chs. 1–35 and that left a decisive imprint on this section of the book.

After a discussion of the meaning of אלילים and spatial rhetoric in First Isaiah in ch. 1, my study proceeds with an analysis of the texts in Isa 1–35 that mention the אלילים. These texts (in chs. 2, 10, 19, and 31) provide points of entry into the broader monotheizing rhetoric of First Isaiah. Chapter 2 examines the rhetoric and literary function of Isa 2:6–22 in which Isaiah's unique rhetoric of exaltation and abasement features. This text plays a defining role for YHWH's political supremacy in First Isaiah. Not only do the אלילים receive mention three times, but the passage also brings the אלילים into collocation with an intense series of spatial claims about YHWH's exaltation (2:11, 17). YHWH's sole divinity is construed in vertical terms. In other words, spatial high/low metaphors set the terms by which YHWH's exaltation is conceptualized. I suggest that Isa 2:6–22 is

---

66. See Aster, *Reflections of Empire*.

deliberately anticipating themes related to divine supremacy that occur throughout Isa 1–35.

Chapter 3 explores the judgment on Assyria in Isa 10. I consider the arrogant boasts of Assyria in Isa 10:9–11, which sit within a prophetic proclamation against the Assyrian king (vv. 5–15) and use the term אלילים. These verses bear striking similarities to Isa 36:18–20, which refer to the nations' *deities* rather than their *images*, as in Isa 10. These verses not only demonstrate an aversion to אלהים in Isa 1–35 but also raise questions about the way that monotheistic rhetoric in chs. 36–39 influenced Isa 10 or vice versa, or whether there is evidence of mutual influence. I also return to the theme of political supremacy with an analysis of the unique divine name האדון in Isa 10:16, 33 and the abasement of YHWH's enemies.

Chapter 4 considers the fascinating uses of אלילים in Isa 19:1–4, an oracle against Egypt. The prophet claims that the Egyptians will consult their אלילים, along with spiritists and mediums, in the day of trouble. However, those alleged sources of knowledge will fail them. This chapter highlights the epistemological import of אלילים language. Though a comparison with 8:19 (and LXX 19:3), moreover, I suggest that Isa 19 refers to the Egyptians' deities as "non-gods," or "fraudulent gods" (אלילים). YHWH asserts his sovereignty (cf. the use of האדון in 19:4) in the face of Egypt's inability to elicit political knowledge from their idols. Isaiah highlights the folly of the idol's political insights, since adherents of אֱלִילִים become אֱוִלִים (fools).

The final chapter draws together the findings of this study and then steps back to consider the relationship between monotheistic rhetoric in First and Second Isaiah. While the two corpora share certain features (e.g., mockery of idols), their lexical choices and modes of monotheizing differ. I also examine places where Deutero-Isaiah may have influenced Proto-Isaiah's rhetoric (e.g., 2:8b, 18; 8:19–21; 21:9) and vice versa.

CHAPTER I

Rhetoric of Exaltation and Abasement in First Isaiah

ONE OF THE DISTINCTIVE FEATURES of First Isaiah is its twin emphasis on YHWH's unparalleled exaltation and the abasement of all else. It is perhaps not surprising that the same book that displays such an emphasis on YHWH's "high and exalted" status as king also relegates other kings to the underworld.[1] Moreover, the same book that asserts YHWH's loftiness also mocks the "gods" as אלילים. Consistently, First Isaiah underscores the idea that YHWH is utterly exalted while all other puffed-up powers will come crashing down. To understand this rhetoric, and its contribution to Isaiah's understanding of YHWH's categorical supremacy, we have to examine two related phenomena: (1) Dysphemistic language related to other deities, with a focus on the אלילים, and (2) spatial rhetoric in the book. This will set the stage for our study of Isa 2:5–22, where both phenomena come into sharp focus.

The אלילים in Isaiah

Meaning and Origins

I suggest that Isa 1–35 displays a reticence to designate any but YHWH as an אלהים, but instead favors the derisive term אלילים. The term אלילים occurs ten times in First Isaiah, and most other uses appear to be later.[2] The specific meaning of the term אלילים has been debated. Ibn Ezra suggested that אלילים had as its root the negative particle אל, indicating that there is "no reality in them."[3] While clearly not accounting for the full orthography or etymology of the root, Ibn Ezra's point captures the point that the term negates the reality implied in the term אלהים.

Most argue that the term אלילים derives from אליל, a singular noun used adjectivally on several occasions and that is often translated "worthless." Some instances of the term אליל convey the idea of fraudulence (Job 13:4; Jer 14:14), given its semantic affiliation with "lies" (e.g., שקר). For instance, Job insists that

---

1. Isaiah 14. See Hays, *Covenant with Death*.
2. Lev 19:4; 26:1; Ezek 30:13; Hab 2:18; Ps 96:5; 97:7; 1 Chr 16:26.
3. Friedländer, *Commentary of Ibn Ezra on Isaiah*, 1:16.

his friends are all "plasterers of lies, and sham healers [רֹפְאֵי אֱלִל]."[4] Jeremiah writes that his opponents were "prophesying false visions, sham divination [וקסם ואליל] and the deceit of their own heart" (Jer 14:14).[5] These texts create a semantic equivalence between אליל deceitfulness, and perhaps more specifically, the deceitfulness and fraudulence of "experts." The friends of Job and prophets of Israel perpetuated false remedies and promises. The singular noun/adjective may have been influenced by First Isaiah's application of the term אליל to idols. Scholars tend to argue that the plural אלילים association with "idols" developed from that singular noun meaning "worthless," but that direction of influence is difficult to determine.

In addition to its possible relation to the singular אליל, scholars rightly note the acoustic similarity between the plural אלילים and אלהים. Williamson suggests that אלילים is a disparaging pun based on the terms for deity (אל and אלהים), perhaps in conjunction with the term for worthless (אליל).[6] He notes that the etymology of the term is difficult to determine with any certainty. Carlton Hodge suggests that both אלהים and אלילים derive from the same root *'il, which were then pluralized according to different processes.[7] He notes that the term אלהים derives from the same Semitic root, but that it reflects the pluralization of the expanded form אֱלוֹהַּ according to the standard Hebrew masculine plural.

The term אלילים, by contrast, may preserve a process of pluralizing the Semitic *'il by reduplication, hence אליל (and eventually אלילים).[8] Marvin Pope notes several reduplicated forms in Old South Arabic and North Arabic, which were applied to deities. One may also note the tendency in the Sargonic period to use "iteration or reduplication of one syllable," especially with divine names, when casting spells.[9] This may explain how the form came about. Uncertainty remains, however, since none of the cited examples of reduplication originate in a time or location close to First Isaiah.

---

4. Assuming that אֱלִל derives from the same root as אֱלִיל. Note the phrase "plasterers of lies" from the CEB.

5. The phrase וקסם ואליל (lit., "and divination and sham") follows the Qere reading. The phrase likely forms a unit, to be read as וקסם אליל ("sham divination") as part of a threefold denunciation of false prophets. This group of three sits in relation to YHWH's threefold statement that "I have not sent them. I have not commanded them. I did not speak to them" earlier in the verse. Note the Ketib reading וְקֶסֶם וֶאֱלוּל.

6. Williamson, *Isaiah 1–5*, 216.

7. Hodge, "Elilim." He also suggests that the אלילים were ancestor images. However, other than arguing that "ancestor images" makes the most sense of the term's various appearances, he does not make a convincing argument. His study depends, in part, on the idea that אלהים are, fundamentally, deceased elders. He compares the אלילים to teraphim that Israelite households would revere.

8. On the development of plurals through reduplication, see Carl Brockelmann, *Grundriß der vergleichenden Grammatik*, 1:439–40 §240, though Brockelmann suggests that the reduplicated 'il'ilt is to be pointed 'alā'ilat.

9. Steiner, *Early Northwest Semitic Serpent Spells*, 16.

Baruch Podolsky argues that the weakness of alternative etymologies commends a return to the older thesis of Gesenius that אליל derives from the Akkadian Illil (= Sumerian *Enlil*). Podolsky suggests that the general decline of the Babylonian deity may have associated him with "weakness," an idea that seems reinforced in Isaiah and elsewhere (Isa 10:10–11). He does not develop the thesis but notes Clay's and Gesenius's arguments to that effect.[10] Christopher B. Hays, as A. T. Clay and Podolsky before him, also argues that אליל derives from the Akkadian Illil and offers the most thorough defense of this etymology. Hays is critical of attempts to root the origins of אלילים in the abstract noun אליל (vanity, worthlessness). He questions the assumption that the plural "worthless *idols*" derived from a singular noun or adjectival base. Hays notes that that the adjective use of אליל emerged late (Zech 11:17; Sir 11:3), and the other purported adjectival uses are spelled differently, אֱלִל in Job 13:4 and אֱלוּל in Jer 14:14. Moreover, he suggests that even these latter texts are late and postdate an earlier meaning of the term.[11]

Hays's claim that occurrences of אליל in Jer 14:14 and Job 13:4 are later than uses in First Isaiah is open to debate. Jeremiah 14:14 is part of a prose section, which many date later than the poetry. However, the assumption that prose is later than poetry has recently come under criticism and can no longer be taken for granted.[12] In any case, the אלילים certainly activate a meaning like worthlessness or fraudulence in its rhetorical contexts in First Isaiah.

Hays argues that אליל originated as the name of the Nippurian deity Enlil (written Illil in syllabic Akkadian).[13] The clearest instance of this form occurs in Isa 10:10, which refers to the "kingdoms of Illil" (לממלכות האליל), the southern Mesopotamian kingdoms conquered by Sennacherib. Sennacherib himself celebrated conquering the southern Mesopotamian regions, including Nippur, home of Enlil/Illil.[14] Sennacherib eventually called *all* those ruled by Assyria "'subjects of the god Illil' (*baʾulāt Illil*)."[15] Hays thus dates Isa 10:10 quite close to Sennacherib's time. He notes, however, that "since the entire point of these proto-Isaianic passages is that YHWH and not the Assyrians (or their gods) was in charge of history, אליל carried the connotation 'false god' from its beginnings" in Isaiah.[16] Hays also observes that because "lordship" was one of Enlil's defining characteristics, additional terms such as "*illilu*, 'god of the highest rank' and *illilūtu*, 'divine supremacy (literally 'Enlil-ship')" developed and were applied

---

10. Podolsky, "Notes on Hebrew Etymology," 203.
11. Hays, "Enlil."
12. Henderson, *Jeremiah*.
13. Hays, "Enlil," 226.
14. Ibid., 231.
15. Ibid., 229.
16. Ibid., 230.

to other deities such as Šamaš, Marduk, Sîn, and Nabû. I would also add that Neo-Assyrian royal inscriptions tend to use Enlil + definite article ("*the* Enlil of the gods") to describe deities besides Enlil.[17] The definite article in Isa 10:10 (with the phrase ממלכות האליל, "kingdoms of *the* Illil") seems to reflect that more generalized use of the term. It need not necessitate an originally specific reference to Enlil the deity in Isaiah.

Hays argues that, although אליל began as a specific designator for Enlil/Illil, it also designated other deities in Isaiah.[18] This happened in Isa 19:3, where the term stands in parallel with *eṭimmu*, a known Akkadian loanword.[19] We read:

They will consult their *'ĕlîlîm* and their shades,
their ghosts and their familiar spirits (19:3b)

ודרשו אל־האלילים ואל־האטים
ואל־האבות ואל־הידענים

Though the mythological link to Enlil is likely lost in this later text, Hays says that it still is used "essentially correctly" to refer to Egyptian divinities in general, just like *eṭimmu* refers to Egyptian spirits of the dead. Thus, for Hays, האלילים in 19:3 refer to divinities, not idols yet, and is an Akkadian-influenced term that functions essentially like אלהים, albeit false ones. After its uses in Isa 10:10 and 19:3, אלילים connoted "idols" in its plural forms.

Hays's study is a helpful corrective to the general assumption that First Isaiah *created* the term אלילים to mock other deities. As he argues, אליל may have *originated* under the influence of the Akkadian Enlil, or at least the generic use of "the Enlil of *x*" as a way of indicating supremacy. I doubt that the connection with Enlil persisted into Isaiah, with the possible exception of Isa 10:10. Even there, the specific association seems muted in favor of a generic use. The plural use of אליל in 10:11 in parallel with עצב (idol) suggests as much for the preceding use in 10:10.[20] The term אלילים marks a kind of "archaic demythologizing," to use Albright's term.[21] Whatever association it may have had with a Babylonian deity in the Assyrian's mouth (10:10), Isaiah (or a later redactor) denies the deity's legitimacy (10:11). First Isaiah may retain the residue of another deity in the singular אליל but presses the term into new meanings with the plural אלילים.

---

17. E.g., RINAP III 35, i 1; 48, o 8; 50, 2', 104, i 34; 104, vii 30; 105, i 37b; 105, x 16; 106, iv 48; 107, x 15'. Many more examples can be found at the University of Pennsylvania's collection of Royal Inscriptions of the Neo-Assyrian Period via http://oracc.museum.upenn.edu/rinap.

18. Hays, "Enlil," 230.

19. Ibid., 230–31.

20. Hays considers 10:11 redactionally later than 10:10 (ibid., 231).

21. Discussed in Hallo, "One God for Many."

One can make a case that the uses of אלילים in First Isaiah are redactionally later than their surrounding contexts, even if a firm date is impossible to fix.[22] Nothing requires us to assume that a singular form occurred first, especially if אלילים is a derisive term based on אלהים, perhaps patterned on the noun פָּסִיל (idol), כְּסִיל (fool), or אֱוִיל (foolish), all of which occur in First Isaiah and share a similar vowel pattern. Hays's study at the very least cautions us against assuming too hastily that אלילים originated from a noun אליל, meaning fraud.

Nevertheless, some broad conclusions can be stated hear about the word אלילים:

1. It is related to the Semitic *'il.
2. The pluralized form seems designed to evoke, albeit in a deformed state, the plural אלהים. Even if not created as such in its singular form, it seems to function in First Isaiah as a mocking dysphemism that enabled First Isaiah to avoid gracing other (non)deities with the label אלהים, to make them disappear *as "gods."*
3. Its *use* in Isaiah and elsewhere activates the association with the abstract noun אליל, meaning vanity/worthlessness. However, it may not be the *origin* of the term, as Hays notes.

Overemphasis on the precise etymological *origins* of the term אליל can obscure the term's *function* in First Isaiah.[23] Understanding the meaning of אלילים in Isaiah requires attention to its rhetorical function in the book. I suggest the use of the term in First Isaiah reflects three primary senses of the word, all of which mock the presumption that idols convey divinity:

1. Unreliability: The אלילים cannot be trusted to deliver what they promise, including reliable knowledge.
2. Fraudulence: The אלילים are not what they appear to be.
3. Foolishness: The אֱלִילִים render their devotees אֱוִלִים ("fools").

I unpack these meanings during my study but note here that these senses of the term emerge in context. They are not discernible based on etymology alone. Nevertheless, the plural אלילים is likely functioning like tabooistic deformations or dysphemisms of the word *God*, used almost exclusively in First Isaiah for Israel's deity.

---

22. See Williamson, "Idols in Isaiah."
23. To be clear, Hays is interested in *both* in his study.

Deformation and Dysphemism

Tabooistic deformations are words designed deliberately to avoid pronouncing certain words considered taboo, because they are either offensive or deemed dangerous to pronounce.[24] Modern examples include *dang* to avoid *damn* or *gosh* instead of *God*. As Brent Strawn points out, such deformations can alter a term's phonetic shape in unpredictable ways.[25] Etymologies for such deformations are difficult. Strawn observes that religious topics are frequent objects of such tabooistic deformations. Notably, "Such changes were to avoid affront to God, on the one hand, but, on the other hand, intentional deformations of outsider terminology could function to disparage foreign entities such as the false gods of the nations."[26] In this sense, it is not only the perceived danger or offense of saying the word but the *folly* of saying certain words. To this extent, tabooistic deformations can function dysphemistically. They can purposely distort a word to mock.

A similar situation seems to obtain with אלילים. While perhaps not originally *designed* to mock, its similarity to the Hebrew אלהים, and use of the common Semitic *'il(u)* → *'ēl*, rendered it ripe for mocking rhetoric. Dyphemism, as Shalom Paul defines is, "is the substitution of an offensive or disparaging term for an inoffensive one."[27] Marvin Pope offers a similar definition, namely, "the use of grossly disparaging terms rather than normal or neutral designations."[28] One tendency in dysphemic terminology is the deliberate corruption of terms. For instance, the deity Beelzebub likely corrupts Beelzebul ("Baal [the] Prince"; 1 Kgs 1:12). As Pope notes, "The element *zĕbub*, apparently onomatopoeic imitation of the buzzing of flies or bees (Isa 7:18)," and may connote excrement.[29] We may also mention the use of בשת (for בעל) in 2 Sam 2:8, 4:4, 11:21, and Jer 3:24. Similarly, Ashtoreth "may be a dysphemism alluding to *boshet*, "shame" (e.g., 1 Kgs 11:5, 33).[30]

In addition, biblical writers substituted derisive terms for places of illicit worship or idol worship. For instance, Hosea refers to Bethel as בית און ("house of iniquity"; 4:15; 5:8; 10:5), and the Deuteronomistic Historian calls Dan's temple

---

24. Strawn, "Etymology of בליעל Once Again," 7.
25. Ibid., 7, 9.
26. Ibid., 10, following Pope, "Euphemism."
27. Shalom M. Paul, "Dysphemism," 550.
28. Pope, "Bible, Euphemism and Dysphemism."
29. Pope, "Euphemism," ad loc. Strawn also highlights the term בליעל/*bĕlîyaʿal*, "Belial," which seems to be a deformed version of Baʿal, which came to predominate in the Dead Sea Scrolls. Strawn, "Etymology of בליעל Once Again," 13–14.
30. Pope, "Euphemism," ad loc.

the בית במות ("temple of Bamot"; 1 Kgs 12:31).³¹ In short, biblical authors developed a sophisticated vocabulary of dysphemisms to condemn and deride idols and places of idol worship and, very likely, to avoid gracing deities with the status of their proper names or status.

But what evidence do we have that First Isaiah *mocks* using the term אלילים? One important body of evidence is the wide range of pluralized dysphemisms in the Old Testament. There is a striking tendency to deride false deities with pluralized terms that are either mocking or negative in connotation. The following examples deserve attention:³²

1. זר, "strange," is pluralized as זרים to describe the non-gods to which Israel sacrificed in Deut 32:16.
2. תועבה, "abomination," is pluralized as תועבות to describe prohibited deities (e.g., Deut 32:16; Ezek 5:9, 11; and elsewhere).
3. שקוץ, "detested thing," is pluralized as שקוצים in frequent reference to idols (Deut 29:16; 2 Kgs 23:24; Jer 7:30; 32:34) or illicit practices (Jer 13:27). It appears frequently in parallel with (תועבות; Jer 16:27; Ezek 5:11; 7:20; 11:18, 21).
4. גל/גלל, "dung" or "heap of stones," is pluralized as גלולים throughout Ezekiel and in Lev 26:30 to describe divine images. Most consider the vocalization of גלולים to be based on שקוצים. ³³
5. קבץ, "to gather," (or קבוץ, "assembly") is pluralized as קבוצים, "collected things," or idol statues in Isa 57:13.³⁴ The plural noun seems to be modeled on שקוצים.
6. אימה, "fright" or "dread," is pluralized as אימים (//פסלים) in Jer 50:38 in mocking description of images (feminine noun אימה typically אימות when referring to "terrors").³⁵
7. מות, "dead (person)," in this case a nominalized verb, is pluralized as מתים in reference to Baal, suggesting that by yoking themselves to Baal at Peor the people had hitched themselves to the dead, possibly a mocking description of Baal idols (Ps 106:28; cf. Num 25:9).

---

31. This translation follows Greer, *Dinner at Dan*, 9. Greer argues convincingly that the plural במות is a Deuteronomistic revision for an original בית יהוה, in reference to the shrine at Dan. Cf. the use of the singular construct + plural noun (בית הבמות) in 2 Kgs 17:29 and 32.

32. For a study of dysphemism in the Hebrew Bible, see Paul, "Dysphemism," 550; Jastrow, "Element בשת."

33. Kutsko, *Between Heaven and Earth*, 33–34. Kutsko includes a helpful discussion of גלולים's etymology.

34. See discussion in *HALOT*, ad loc; Goldingay, *Isaiah 56–66*, 97.

35. In Jer 50:38, אימים stands in parallel to פסלים, just as אלילים is brought into comparison with the פסילים in Isa 10:10–11.

8. הבל, "vapor, breath," is pluralized as הבלים in Jer 8:19, 10:8, and 14:22 to describe foreign idols, and in 23:16, as a *hiphil* verb to describe the "befooling" or "deluding" words of false prophets.
9. תעה/תעע, "to mock/wander," is the likely verbal root of the nominal תעתעים in Jer 10:15 and 51:18 and describes the idols of Babylon.

We could add to these examples other terms that employ singular forms to create derisive terminology for idols or deities. For instance, a narrator of Kings refers to Milcom and Chemosh "the detestable object(s) (שקוץ) of" Ammon and Moab rather than calling them the *gods* of Ammon and Moab (cf. Dan 11:31). The tendency to pluralize suggests that biblical writers perceive the sheer *number* of idols or gods problematic. The mockery and critique highlight the problem of divine plurality.

At times, these dysphemisms draw particularly odious portraits of idolatry. Ezekiel's use of גלולים, "dung clods," illustrates how idols defile Israel and the temple. As a double entendre also suggesting "stone heaps," the term also illustrates the ways that idols are mere stones.[36] These are "Sheissgötter"—both defiling and fake.[37] Jeremiah calls images אימים, or "frights," because they lead the people into a frightening and dangerous drought (Jer 50:38). To return to First Isaiah, we may ask what meaning and function the prophet lends the term אלילים in First Isaiah. In its most straightforward sense, אלילים demonstrates the aural similarity between אלהים and אלילים. The fraudulent nature of the אלילים is apparent based on orthographic similarity with אלהים. Moreover, depending on the time in which it was used, it could activate either associations with the defeated "kingdoms of Enlil" (10:10) or the notion of falsehood signaled by the term אליל.

This derisive use of אלילים trades on the alleged sense of security and help that images were supposed to provide their worshipers. In the context of First Isaiah, of course, the commitment to images was closely related to reliance on foreign power, as argued above. As the people form alliances with other nations, and through them, seek security, the prophet exclaims that the people have attached themselves to frauds. Further evidence for a dysphemic reading of אלילים will emerge during this study.

Finally, I note that First Isaiah exhibits a unique range of terms for illicit objects of cultic devotion. I have outlined these in appendix 1, where the difference in terminology between First and Second Isaiah can be observed.[38] First Isaiah includes a range of terminology that never occurs in Isa 40–55.

---

36. Kutsko, *Between Heaven and Earth*, 34.
37. Wolff, "Jahwe und die Götter," 407, cited in Kutsko, *Between Heaven and Earth*, 34.
38. For a discussion of some terminological differences, see Williamson, "Idols in Isaiah."

These include terms such as אלילים ("fraud gods"), מעשה ידים ("works of [your] hands"), מזבחות ("altars"), and חמנים ("incense altars"). Other terms exhibit consistent orthographic differences. For instance, First Isaiah prefers פסיל to פסל. Furthermore, Deutero- (and to some extent, Trito-) Isaiah has its own terminology related to illicit objects of cultic devotion that do not overlap with First Isaiah.

Exaltation and Abasement in First Isaiah

In addition to mocking the alleged divinity of the "gods," Isaiah exhibits a striking emphasis on YHWH's exaltation and the simultaneous abasement of all that elevates itself. The deformative rhetoric around the gods is matched by the debasing rhetoric the prophet so consistently deploys for other powers. This second major area of investigation is important for my study. It answers the question *What are the terms by which First Isaiah conceptualizes YHWH's categorical supremacy?* This question allows for Isaiah's own descriptive categories for understanding First Isaian monotheism, rather than squeezing the book into an ill-fitting mold and asking it to yield a verdict on the question *How many deities populate the heavens?* A purely quantitative approach to monotheism is nonsensical. It merely addresses the population of what many biblical writers considered part of the created realm. But First Isaiah's unique poetics ignore the question of deities in the heavens and instead pits YHWH's supreme power against all else that raises itself up. In other words, First Isaiah's is a spatial conception of supremacy.[39]

Spatial Metaphor and Rhetoric

Traversing the rhetorical terrain of First Isaiah forces readers to crane their necks regularly to look upward at the impressive summits the poet describes, and at times, to stare down mountain into the disappearing depths of the canyons below. The experience of First Isaiah is like visiting the giant redwoods of Northern California. Visiting Redwood National Park inevitably draws visitors' attention to the stunning and seemingly impossible vertices that fill the park, already set in the mountain heights. The experience of redwood grandeur is vertically construed. It would be silly to talk about the *sprawling* nature of the redwoods without any reference to their height. Similarly, it would be odd to

---

39. One could also argue that other rhetorical categories obtain for the prophet, but those lie outside the scope of this study. For instance, YHWH's overwhelming *glory* and *holiness* constitutes a major aspect of the prophet's rhetoric of divine supremacy.

talk about the stunning vertical lines of the Great Wall of China. The "greatness" of that wall is horizontally conceived. The fact that it traverses high mountains notwithstanding, the Great Wall achieves its wonder and admiration because of the length of its ancient fortification walls. Compare the vertically conceived language of Isaiah—"YHWH alone will be *exalted on high* in that day" (Isa 2:11, 12, 17)—with the horizontally construed description of Solomon's wisdom— "God gave Solomon wisdom and very great understanding, insight *as long as the seashore itself*" (1 Kgs 4:29).[40] Solomon's unmatched wisdom depends on the conceptual metaphor GREATNESS AS BREADTH. First Isaiah, by contrast, deploys a set of metaphors drawn from a construal of SUPREMACY AS HEIGHT.[41]

Isaiah's conception of divine grandeur is vertically conceived. While other modes of rhapsodizing YHWH's greatness populate chs. 1–39, the lofty nature of YHWH and his categorical opposition to all that strives for loftiness is the prophet's primary mode of articulating divine supremacy. The lofty throne scene in Isa 6 is thus an appropriate entrée into the conceptual world of First Isaian theological rhetoric. The prophet encounters YHWH at the temple, "high and lifted up." He is enthroned on high. Spatially, the furniture in the temple did not work that way. The covenant chest was on level ground with the holy place. But Isaiah never mentions the ark, only the cherubim's winged cousins that hovered over the ark. In Isaiah's recounting, the temple was a visionary gateway to the heavenly realms that intersected with earth, which drew eyes upward to the king on high. The fringe of the divine garment alone was sufficient to fill the temple. In other words, the lowest viewable element of the divine was enough to fill a temple. The imagery begs for only the loftiest imaginings.

Understanding First Isaiah's vertically conceived theological convictions requires attention to the range and distribution of terms employed. The range and distribution of spatial terminology suggests that a "megametaphor" is at work in First Isaiah. Megametaphors, or extended root metaphors, provide underlying coherence to a range of surface metaphors that appear throughout a work. If YHWH's exalted throne is a focal image for divine rule, then SUPREMACY AS HEIGHT is the metaphor that integrates First Isaiah's theological claims. As Zoltan Kovecses points out, megametaphors (like all conceptual metaphors) are often hidden. Isaiah does not say "SUPREMACY IS HEIGHT" or "THE HIGHEST HEIGHTS ARE THE MOST POWERFUL." Instead, what surfaces are a range of surface metaphors that are explained in terms of the underlying root metaphor

---

40. Thanks to Brent Strawn for the 1 Kgs 4:29 example, taken from the CEB, with emphasis added (as in the previous quotation).

41. On conceptual vs. metaphorical linguistic expressions, see Kovecses, *Metaphor*, 4–7. There are limits to the "x *as* y" or "x *is* y" approach to metaphor, since not all metaphorical construals permit such comparative representations. However, for this study, the conceptualization of SUPREMACY AS HEIGHT fits the kind of imagery First Isaiah employs. See Heim, *Adoption*, 37–38.

SUPREMACY AS HEIGHT.[42] This metaphor draws from a spatial cognitive pattern according to which *up* is powerful and *down* is weak. Here are just a few of the many examples from First Isaiah:

> YHWH alone will be *exalted on high* in that day (Isa 2:11, 12, 17)
> YHWH of Hosts will be *elevated* in justice (Isa 5:16).
> I saw the sovereign sitting on a throne, *high and exalted* (Isa 6:1)
> Proclaim that his [YHWH's] name is *exalted on high* (Isa 12:4)
> "Now I will *arise*," says YHWH,
> > "Now I will *raise myself up*,
> > Now I will *be lifted up*." (Isa 30:33)
>
> YHWH is *exalted on high*, for he *dwells on the heights* (Isa 33:5)

Alongside these texts that emphasize YHWH's elevated status are those that refer to the abasement of all that raises itself up. The downfall of other self-aggrandizing powers forms a natural complement to the images of YHWH in the heights. The SUPREMACY AS HEIGHT metaphor is conceptualized in a way that bars any possibility of shared heights.[43] It is an exclusive height. "Up high" is a place for one occupant, like a steep-sided mountain peak. Thus, self-elevation of other powers is inherently incompatible with YHWH's status. The metaphor's imagery depends on the reader's buy-in on this idea. This opposition sets the stage for First Isaiah to dramatize the ruin of YHWH's opponents.

> The eyes of the proud (lit., *lofty*) human will be *made low*,
> the *elevated* (status) of men will be *abased* (Isa 2:11; cf. 2:9, 12, 17)
> Jerusalem has *stumbled*, Judah has *fallen* (Isa 3:8)
> The *tallest* (trees) on the *heights* will be *hewn down*,
> and the *loftiest* will be *laid low* (10:33; cf. v. 34)
> You will be *brought down* to Sheol,
> to the innermost parts of the *pit* (Isa 14:15).
> The earth will *fall*, and never again *rise* (Isa 24:20).
> On every mountain and *height*,
> and upon every *high* and *raised up place*,
> will be streams of running water,
> on the great day of slaughter,
> when towers *fall*. (Isa 30:25)

---

42. Kovecses, *Metaphor*, 57–58.
43. Unless YHWH raises them up, a point to which Trito-Isaiah returns (Isa 52:13; 57:15; 66:1–2).

For First Isaiah, self-elevating powers—whether nations or individuals—will be reduced before the incomparably exalted YHWH. The demotion and abasement of other powers or individuals underscores the point that, for First Isaiah, the heights allowed none other but YHWH. Moreover, human attempts to elevate themselves were inherently illusory. Thus, in 2:11 it is the "eyes" of humanity that are abased, and in v. 17 their "pride" is cast down. The incongruence of humanity *actually* dwelling on the heights through self-ambition may explain the unusual construction in 2:12: "For YHWH of Hosts has a day against all that is high and lofty, and against all that is lifted, *and it will be abased*." The abasement is so inevitable that the writer includes this final assurance, even if by means of awkward syntax.[44]

Nature and Frequency of Spatial Metaphors

Spatial metaphors of divine loftiness are pervasive in First Isaiah. Given the frequency of this spatial rhetoric, it is surprising that this rhetoric has not received more attention.[45] I will offer an introduction to this rhetoric, before highlighting its significance for the present study. Appendix 2 details some of the most significant spatial terminology related to exaltation (or height) and abasement (or depths), insofar as they related to YHWH or that which is opposed to him.[46]

Isaian scholarship has rightly emphasized the importance of YHWH's "high and exalted" throne vision (Isa 6:1). It occupies an important place in the book's final form. It sits at the juncture between the judgment oracles of Isa 1–5 and the prophecies concerning kingship in Isa 7–12. The lofty throne motif functions in Isaiah, as it does throughout the ancient world, as a means of exemplifying a deity's status and power.[47] The scene's emphasis on praising attendants, glory, and royal garments contributes to a sense of wonder at YHWH's supremacy and constitutes an implicit critique of Assyrian throne rooms that Israel's ambassadors would have frequented.[48] The scene—with its strong royal motifs—provides a theological basis for the sharp division between the realms of human and divine rule marked out thus far in the book.[49] The centrality of YHWH's "high and exalted" throne commends an attempt to consider the book's spatial rhetoric.

---

44. For an alternative assessment of this syntax, see Barré, "Rhetorical-Critical Study," 522–24.
45. An exception is Kyun Chul Paul Kim's study "Little Highs, Little Lows"; see also Archibald L. H. M. van Wieringen's discussion of the "High/Low" theme in Isa 24:21–25:12 in his essay "Isaiah 24:21–25:12," 81–86; Sweeney, *Isaiah 1–39*, 89, 100–102.
46. Pp. 108–9.
47. Metzger, *Königsthron und Gottesthron*; Brettler, *God Is King*.
48. Aster, *Reflections of Empire*, 41–80.
49. Childs, *Isaiah*, 55.

Several scholars have noted the prevalence of "high" and "low" language in Isaiah. Kyun Chul Paul Kim traces the broad contours of such rhetoric through the whole book.[50] His synchronic approach notes the continuation of some terminology throughout Isaiah. He notes the sharp political tone of Isaiah's spatial rhetoric. YHWH opposes the haughty rulers of his people (5:15–16; chs. 28–29) and makes the nations' rulers fall (chs. 13–23). In several places, Isaiah extends his critique to include *any* self-exalted power (chs. 2, 24–27).[51] Kim pays less attention to some of the unique spatial terminology in First Isaiah and to the far more frequent use of such language in that section of the book.

I highlight here several key features of First Isaiah's spatial rhetoric and will develop these points in the chapters that follow. First, certain spatial terms are either mostly or entirely concentrated in First Isaiah. For instance, the verb *שׂגב ("to exalt") occurs in Isa 2, 9, 12, 26, 30, and 33 but never in Deutero-Isaiah.[52] Similarly, *שחח ("to be low") occurs only in First Isaiah. Other terms occur almost exclusively in First Isaiah but also in Isa 40 (e.g., *עלה and *שפל).[53] The presence of these terms in First Isaiah and Isa 40 aligns with the idea that Isa 40 is a bridge between the book's major sections. On other occasions, First Isaiah extends the familiar spatial lexicon. Speaking of the unjust city, Isaiah claims that "the city will be utterly flattened" (וּבַשִּׁפְלָה תִּשְׁפַּל הָעִיר, 32:19). The noun שִׁפְלָה is a hapax legomenon, derived here from the root *שפל. First Isaiah has a particular fondness for this root, employing it at least 17 times, with only two occurrences in the rest of Isaiah.

Second, each spatial term relating to of exaltation and abasement occurs far more frequently in First Isaiah than in other parts of the book. Through repeated use of metaphors, drawn from the conceptual metaphor SUPREMACY AS HEIGHT, First Isaiah confronts readers with the reality that YHWH is not only exalted but also intolerant of others who raise themselves up. For analysis (in appendix 2), I selected the main spatial terms that occur throughout the book of Isaiah, defining this terminology in terms of rhetoric that emphasized YHWH's elevated status, the elevation of others, or the abasement of anything else in relation to YHWH. If a particular term was used in a nonspatial sense (e.g., *קום used to refer to YHWH's word "standing"), I did not include it. I focused on up-down expressions related to YHWH's rising, his opponents' rising, or the abasement of others.[54] Of those spatial terms analyzed (in appendix 2), there

---

50. Kim, "Little Highs, Little Lows."
51. Ibid., 135–47.
52. Isa 2:11, 17; 9:10; 12:4; 26:5; 30:13; 33:5. See *HALOT*, ad loc.
53. The latter also occurs in Isa 57. One could make a case for including *כשׁל ("to stumble"), which occurs in parallel with *נפל on several occasions. It occurs eleven times in Isaiah, six of which are in First Isaiah and two in Isa 40:30.
54. Some "borderline" terms were excluded but would add further support. See, e.g., *רמס ("to trample"), used in Isa 1:12; 16:4; 26:6; 28:3; 41:25; 63:3.

were 133 occurrences in First Isaiah compared to only 26 in Deutero-Isaiah and 20 in Trito-Isaiah. The difference is striking. Spatial rhetoric related to YHWH's exaltation and the abasement of opponents is clearly a distinctive feature of First Isaiah. First Isaiah's theology of exaltation is vertically construed.

In addition to specific spatial terms, one could also extend the analysis to include spatial imagery in the book that emphasizes YHWH's height through other means. For instance, the heavy use of "mountain" terminology in Isaiah—more than any other book in the Old Testament—sets the book on rhetorical terrain that emphasizes height and depth.[55] One may also consider the contrasting "heaven" and "earth" rhetoric, or the emphasis on abasing kings in the underworld.[56] The root metaphor SUPREMACY AS HEIGHT also gives rise to various derivative metaphors to describe what YHWH opposes, such as "cedars," "high mountains," "high tower," and "fortification wall" (2:12–17; 10:33–34; 14:8; 37:24). Because these metaphors are *poetic* metaphors, we should not be surprised by their sheer diversity. At times, this diversity involves using metaphorical images that activate different elements of the root metaphor, such as the merchant ships (2:16). The merchant ships lend an economic hue to the prophetic critique, while still implying the sense of height with the tall masts of ships (juxtaposed here to the tall cedars and oaks).[57]

Third, spatial terminology is structurally significant. The key term *רום, which occurs in Isaiah's throne scene, appears in the first poetic verse: "Children I reared (*רום), I raised *them*, but they rebelled against me!" (1:2). In response to such rebellion, YHWH raises himself up (33:10). As Hays notes, "The theme of bringing low versus raising up is found in every corner of the book."[58] The most significant finding for this study is the concentration of terms in Isa 2. In addition to the three uses of spatial terms in 2:1–4, we see a stunning twenty-one occurrences of seven different spatial terms in 2:5–22.[59] As I argue in the next chapter, this section provides interpreters with a focal lens for understanding YHWH's status. Moreover, it is also the section where אלילים occurs four times. The reduction of deities to non-deities or idols accompanies God's categorical reduction of other "raised up" forces and YHWH's lofty exaltation. Other sections of First Isaiah also feature exaltation and abasement language. Isaiah 10:5–19 uses spatial terminology five times to describe YHWH's opposition to

---

55. Forms of גבר occur fifty-seven times in Isaiah, more than any other OT book, and about ten percent of all biblical occurrences.

56. *"Heaven and earth"*: see Kim, "Little Highs," 143; *kings in the underworld*: see Hays, *Covenant with Death*.

57. Couey, *Reading the Poetry*, 146; Barré, "Rhetorical-Critical Study," 525, notes Ezek 27:5: "They took a *cedar from Lebanon* to make a *mast* for you" (emphasis original).

58. Hays, *Origins of Isaiah 24–27*, 242.

59. Spatial terms occur eleven times in Isa 10 (5× in vv. 5–19 and 6× in vv. 24–34) and 10× in 14:11–19.

Assyria, YHWH's staff, which vaunts itself against the one who raises it up. Similarly, Isa 14:3–27 uses spatial terms 12 times to describe how the Babylonian king sought to ascend to the "heights," and even raised his throne to the heavenly realm but was cast down to the earth. Further, clusters of spatial terms occur in Isa 30 (6×), which describes the abasement of Egypt and elevation of YHWH as judge.

Finally, by employing the SUPREMACY AS HEIGHT root metaphor, Isaiah not only *describes* YHWH but also *creates* a certain perception of YHWH's status and authority. The metaphor has a persuasive function. As Erin Heim notes, "Metaphors themselves are active agents that create and structure their interpreter's perception of reality." The power of metaphor is its ability to help construct interpreters' perception of the world. An organizing metaphor such as SUPREMACY AS HEIGHT is an appeal to see YHWH in elevated terms, and to perceive the world in relation to YHWH's supremely elevated status. The use of such organizing metaphors creates a wider field of discourse in which the interpreter is invited to participate through acts that reinforce the elevated status of YHWH. It also shapes the hopes of those who adopt Isaiah's discourse. In First Isaiah, this discourse involves an invitation to "go up" to Zion (Isa 2:1–5), to anticipate the spectacular ascent and downfall of Tyre (Isa 14), and to join Isaiah in worship of the "high and exalted" deity (Isa 6).[60]

The metaphor SUPREMACY AS HEIGHT also invites hearers to think of YHWH's exaltation in *exclusive* terms. If height is supreme, and not just powerful, that height permits no other occupants.[61] YHWH is not just "up high" with others. He *alone* is up high. First Isaiah's oppositional discourse around the high/low metaphors helps reinforce this point. No passage does this more forcefully than the short poem in Isa 2:12–17, where the prophet highlights YHWH's "day" against *all* that is high and lofty. The totalizing rhetoric describes *how* YHWH is high. He is up high in the sense that puts him into conflict with all else that elevates itself to the heights. The oppositional qualities of the high/low metaphorical field shapes expectations and highlights certain aspects of YHWH's height. This is part of the function of metaphors. They highlight and hide. In Isaiah, the SUPREMACY AS HEIGHT metaphor highlights the fact that being up high is an utterly exclusive status. It hides—in a rhetorical sense—the fact that in the natural world many heights can, in fact, be shared places, or that conceivably, power could be expressed by going down.[62] The metaphor asks us to look through a field of vision within which supreme power is expressed

---

60. Heim, *Adoption*, 80.
61. Trito-Isaiah develops this theme by introducing the idea that YHWH elevates others to himself (Isa 52:13; 57:15).
62. Heim, *Adoption*, 84–86.

in vertical terms. Especially after 2:12–17, the root metaphor asks us to *expect* conflict anytime someone other than YHWH takes to the heights (e.g., Isa 10, 14). We are also invited to expect that the אלילים, whose very name resembles אלהים, should be cast down to the lowest places—where they disappear from our field of vision (Isa 2:19). It is in these ways that First Isaiah monotheizes.

CHAPTER 2

Yahweh's Exaltation in Isaiah 2:6–22

ISAIAH 1:1–2:5 FOCUSES ALMOST EXCLUSIVELY on the corruption and ultimate renewal of Zion,[1] with only occasional nods toward YHWH's power and authority.[2] But in 2:6–22 the prophet brings YHWH's royal splendor and exalted status into clear focus. The prophet exclaims twice that "YHWH alone will be exalted on that day" (vv. 11, 17) and thrice that YHWH's splendor and glory would "terrify" his foes (vv. 10, 19, 21). As a by-product of the prophet's shift toward divine splendor and supremacy, human pride receives its due. The contrast between the ascent of the nations to Zion in 2:1–5 and the "descent" of humanity in 2:6–22 is striking. Whereas the nations ascend Zion to learn torah, in 2:6–22 humans "bow down" to the work of their hands. Because of this, humanity "is abased and man brought low" (3×, vv. 9, 11, 17). Cast down, they discard their fraudulent deities in caves and holes in the ground (vv. 19–21), the lowest possible places. Thus, as YHWH is exalted, humanity is abased, and false gods are relegated to the realm of death. These three movements go hand in hand.

The importance of 2:6–22 for Isaiah's theology can hardly be overstated. It is the first extended reflection on divine power and exaltation in the book. It is also the first time Isaiah mentions YHWH's "day," and for that matter, it is its first mention (canonically speaking) in the entire prophetic corpus.[3] In addition, the passage's influence extends into other portions of First Isaiah, particularly its theme of divine exaltation (2:6–22). To provide examples: Isaiah's stunning image of YHWH's lofty and exalted throne in 6:1 draws very clearly from the pairing of נשא + רום that occurs three times in ch. 2 (vv. 12, 13, and 14).[4] This theme plays a major role in the developing traditions in First Isaiah and is one of the pillars of Isaiah's proclamation.[5] Isaiah 5 returns to the theme of YHWH's being "exalted in that day" (5:15), language that occurs nowhere else in the

---

1. Isa 2:6–22 also stands between two Zion-exaltation texts (2:1–5; 4:2–6) that play a key role in the books developing theme of Zion as YHWH's "showcase" city, and belongs to 2:1–5 via the linking phrase "house of Jacob" (in vv. 5 and 6). On the redactional function of v. 6a, see Blenkinsopp, *Isaiah 1–39*, 195; Beuken, *Jesaja 1–12*, 99, 102.
2. The one exception is the overloaded divine name in 1:24 (יהוה אלהים צבאות אביר ישראל). I will discuss this name toward the end of ch. 2.
3. While Isa 2:2 mentions "in the latter days" (באחרית הימים), and even 2:11 "in that day" (ביום ההוא), it is only in 2:12 that the prophet uses "day" in a more specific, and arguably deliberately ominous, way: "For YHWH of hosts has a day" (כי יום יהוה צבאות). For similar uses, cf. Isa 13:6, 9.
4. On the relationship between Isa 2 and 6, see Williamson, *Book Called Isaiah*.
5. Berges and Beuken, *Das Buch Jesaja*, 18. Cf. 3:16–24; 6:1; 9:8; 10:12, 33; 13:11, 19; 14:11, 13; 16:6; 23:9; 25:11; 28:1, 3; 37:23.

book. The theme of divine "terror" (vv. 10, 19, 21) reappears in 8:12–13, where the prophet warns the people of Judah to turn from fearing the terror of the Syro-Ephraimite alliance to fearing the terror of YHWH: "Let him be your dread [והוא מערצכם]."[6] Moreover, the prose additions about humanity dispensing with idols before YHWH's overwhelming glory (2:18, 20) anticipate similar idol-focused prose additions in 17:7–8, 30:19–20, and 31:6–7.[7]

Due to its prime literary location and influence in the book, this passage warrants attention, particularly so given this book's emphasis on divine supremacy and what I call the "disappearance of the gods." Isaiah 2:6–22 paints a totalizing portrait of YHWH's supremacy that is every bit as monotheistic as what we find in Isa 40–55. The difference between First and Second Isaiah on monotheism is one of rhetorical modes and not degree. In First Isaiah, YHWH is not just a powerful deity; he relegates to the dust any who would rise in arrogance before him, which includes both human aspirants and divine pretenders. Humans are mortified and so-called deities stripped of their status such that they disappear from memory. I will develop this argument by examining (1) the poetry of 2:6–22, (2) the spatialized rhetoric of exaltation and abasement, and (3) the use of derisive terms for non-deities.

Isaiah 2:6–22: Poetics and Composition

Isaiah 2:6–22 likely underwent a complex redactional process that saw it eventually nested between the vision of a renewed Zion (2:1–5) and a vision of judgment on Jerusalem (3:1–26). The particle כי in 2:6 and 22 and then in 3:1 links Isa 2:6–22 to the next chapter.[8] The precise logic undergirding its current arrangement continues to evade interpreters. Attempts to read 2:6–22 in terms of a carefully crafted literary structure are often forced and ultimately unpersuasive.[9] Brevard Childs says of such attempts that "one gains the impression of an interpreter forcing Shakespeare's rules for composing a sonnet upon the wild and unruly poetry of Walt Whitman."[10] Likewise Blenkinsopp, following

---

6. The verbal root *ערץ occurs in Isa 2:19, 21; 8:12–13; 29:23; 47:12 in Isaiah. On the possible relationship between Isa 2 and the Syro-Ephraimite war, see Roberts, "Isaiah 2."

7. See Blenkinsopp, "Fragments," 54–55. Blenkinsopp argues that the core eighth-century prophecies (vv. 6–8, 10, 12–16) were expanded with texts that both interpret YHWH's judgment in an eschatological framework and critique idolatry.

8. Sweeney, *Isaiah 1–4*, 139.

9. Sweeney's broad structural observations are nonetheless helpful, namely, that (1) vv. 6–9 address YHWH and acknowledge guilt, (2) vv. 10–21 address the people and announce judgment, and (3) v. 22 addresses the reader with a wisdom lesson (*Isaiah 1–4*, 146).

10. Childs, *Isaiah*, ad loc.

Duhm, states that Isa 2:6–22 "is among the most imperfectly preserved passages in the entire collection and also one of the least amenable to regular prosodic analysis."[11]

Rather than a clearly discernible literary structure—the pursuit of which often runs the risk of anachronism—the poetic fragments in 2:6–22 coalesce around two primary portions of text, a prophetic indictment in vv. 6–8 and the verdict in vv. 12–16.[12] To these cling additional poetic and prose texts like iron filings to a magnet. They draw together through several lexical links and thematic emphases. While lacking the type of structure that lends itself to outlining, its texts nonetheless move in concert, and to good rhetorical effect. As Childs writes of 2:6–22:

> [It] produces the effect of a tremendous orchestration of sounds. The drum beat of "full of . . . full of . . . full of . . ." [vv. 6–8] is broken by an alternate cadence of "low, humble, hide." Then again the notes shift to profile the "proud, high, and lofty," which are then shattered in a crescendo of crashing sounds as God rises to terrify the earth, and the Lord alone is glorified in that day. A major criticism of all the various literary reconstructions is that, in the end, the readings are pale and insipid in contrast to the rough, awesome terror produced by the received text.[13]

Childs's assessment suggests that the power of the passage's assertions derives not from abstract claims about divinity. Rather, it derives from the prophet's ability to elicit a response of idol abandonment before YHWH as he "rises to terrify the earth." As YHWH rises and approaches in military step, all is laid low.

The drumbeat Childs describes can be felt powerfully in the pounding repetition of vv. 12–16. Here, the poet uses the anaphoric על twice in each couplet of the five verses to announce YHWH's day against all that is raised up.[14] And to the rhythm of each falling footstep of YHWH's approach grows an increasingly clear sense of his unwillingness to share the lofty realms of the earth, those places to which the proud tend to aspire. He is decidedly against all that is raised up, including the cedars of Lebanon, oaks of Bashan, mountains, hills, towers, fortified walls, ships, and boats (vv. 13–16). YHWH's eschatological day will result in his sole exaltation: "and YHWH alone will be exalted in that day" (ונשגב יהוה

---

11. Blenkinsopp, "Fragments," 51; Kaiser, *Isaiah 1–12*, 58.
12. Cf. Blenkinsopp, "Fragments," 51. Blenkinsopp notes that v. 10 functions as a link between the indictment and verdict (p. 55). Barré, "Rhetorical-Critical Study," makes a good case for including v. 17, such that the unit runs from vv. 12–17 and is arranged chiastically.
13. Childs, *Isaiah*, 33.
14. On the use of anaphora, with special attention to First Isaiah, see Couey, *Reading the Poetry*, 33–34.

לבדו ביום ההוא), a phrase repeated twice in the passage (vv. 11, 17). The coordination of YHWH's opposition to things elevated and his eschatological exaltation signals a combative form of theological absolutizing, as though one makes the other inevitable. For this poet—and indeed for much of First Isaiah—YHWH's categorical supremacy finds expression through a spatial rhetoric of exaltation and abasement.

Spatial Rhetoric in 2:6–22

This section will continue with an analysis of spatial rhetoric in 2:6–22, before examining the prophet's accompanying use of אלילים. As suggested already, the disappearance of deities for First Isaiah is derivative of YHWH's exaltation. The eschatological revelation of YHWH's glory and exaltation will dissolve all competing allegiances and expose as fraudulent all that humans elevate to the place of YHWH. I suggest that part of the "deities-as-fraudulent" rhetoric in First of Isaiah is the avoidance of terminology lending those so-called deities legitimacy, hence the derisive אלילים.

First Isaiah's insistence on leveling the opposition to YHWH sits against the backdrop of two coordinated claims. First, YHWH's city, Zion, "will be the highest (בראש) of the mountains" and "will be lifted up (*נשא) above the hills" (2:2). Many see the Zion traditions in Isaiah, and especially 2:1–5 postdating most of 2:6–22, in which case YHWH's exaltation may be seen as the *cause* of, or at least a precursor to, Zion's exaltation. The theme of Zion's "lifting up" plays a relatively minor role in the book, though numerous texts presuppose its significance as a mountain (cf. Isa 4:2–6; 11:9; 40:9). Second, the rhetorical hostility against things raised up sits against the backdrop of YHWH's own exaltation, a significant theme in chs. 1–39. In this section, we witness a concerted development of the SUPREMACY AS HEIGHT metaphor.

The Lofty Day of YHWH in 2:12–17

To understand Isaiah's spatial rhetoric of divine exaltation better, we turn to the "Day of YHWH" poem in 2:12–17. The poem in 2:12–17 is unique within the book of Isaiah, and within the Old Testament more broadly. The prophet focuses on YHWH's opposition to the loftiness of the natural world (vv. 12–14) and objects of human trust (vv. 14–16). Its tenfold repetition of the preposition על communicates that opposition in stark terms. The opposition results in comprehensive abasement. In what follows, I have underlined the language of abasement, and rhetoric of elevation is in italic type. We read:

(12) For YHWH of hosts has a day	כי יום ליהוה צבאות
against all that is *high* and *lofty*,	על כל־גאה ורם
and against all that is *lifted*,	ועל כל־נשא
(but it will be <u>brought low</u>)	ושפל
(13) Against all the cedars of Lebanon,	ועל כל־ארזי הלבנון
high and *lifted up*	הרמים והנשאים
against all the oaks of Bashan,	ועל כל־אלוני הבשן
(14) Against all the *high* mountains,	ועל כל־ההרים הרמים
against all *raised up* hills,	ועל כל־הגבעות הנשאות
(15) Against every *high* tower,	ועל כל־מגדל גבה
against every fortified wall,	ועל כל־חומה בצורה
(16) Against every ship of Tarshish,	ועל כל־אניות תרשיש
against every desired water vessel.	ועל כל־שכיות החמדה

The poetry drips with spatial rhetoric. Barré observes the recurrence of three primary verbal roots—גבה, רום, נשא—each pertaining to height. Except for רום, which occurs four times, each verb repeats three times in the poem.[15] The reader is led through a series of elevated foes that YHWH brings low, as though trampling an enemy on military campaign. YHWH's theophanic arrival appears to originate from the north and move south, with the "high mountains" in v. 14 suggesting Jerusalem in its present context.[16] Yet, precise coordinates are lacking, giving the poem a more generic and potentially timeless feel. The Lebanon, Bashan, and Tarshish are certainly specific localities, but they may be representative of the *kind* of grandiose opponents YHWH tramples.[17] Roberts argues, alternatively, that the reference to ships from Tarshish and watercraft from Arabia (v. 16) suggests "Yahweh's universal supremacy" from east to west.[18] Perhaps the goal of the geographic reference points is to demonstrate YHWH's supremacy from north to south and from east to west. To the extent the poem is about *all* that is raised up, the geography makes the point.

Oddly, except for the parenthetical aside in v. 12, the brief poem in vv. 12–17 never states clearly that any of the listed objects are "brought low." For that, one has to look at the poetic (and prosaic) verses that frame this theophanic poem. There one finds a dense clustering of abasement rhetoric. It is humanity that YHWH brings low:

---

15. Barré, "Rhetorical-Critical Study," 531–32.
16. Blenkinsopp, "Fragments," 56.
17. Cf. The pairing of Lebanon and Bashan in Isa 33:9; Jer 22:20; Nah 1:4.
18. Following Roberts's rendering of החמדה as a place name (Roberts, *First Isaiah*, 38, 47).

(9) So humanity is <u>abased</u>
and man <u>brought low</u>,
but do not *lift* them!
(11) The eyes of *lofty* humanity will
be <u>brought low</u>, and the *height* of
men <u>abased</u>,
but YHWH alone will be *unattainably high* in that day.
(17) The *loftiness* of humanity will
be <u>abased</u>
and the *height* of men <u>brought low</u>,
But YHWH alone will be *unattainably high* in that day.

וישח אדם
וישפל־איש
ואל־תשא להם
עיני גבהות אדם שפל
ושח רום אנשים
ונשגב יהוה לבדו ביום ההוא

ושח גבהות האדם
ושפל רום אנשים
ונשגב יהוה לבדו ביום ההוא

Verses 12–16 address YHWH's day against all that is "lofty" (גאה), "high" (*רום), and "lifted" (*נשא), and clearly attract these framing verses. But together, vv. 9–11 and 17 perform an interpretive role. They claim that YHWH's war campaign was against the lofty pride of humanity. In fact, the framing verses seem to influence the poem itself, stitching the two together, as it were, with the clause ושפל, "and they will be brought low," in v. 12. The effect of this frame is to specify that the primary object of YHWH's campaign is *humanity*, and that in the face of human attempts at loftiness, YHWH would be raised high.

The latter verse in the frame (v. 17) serves as a concluding bridge between the hard-hitting divine campaign in vv. 12–16 and the material that follows. After the tri-fold repetition of terminology for height (גבה, רום, נשא), the use of the verb נשגב (*niphal*, "to be exalted") is surprising. Barré argues convincingly that, while semantically disjunctive, the נש־ recalls the first syllable of נשא in vv. 12–13, while the גב־ recalls the first part of גבה in vv. 12 and 15. This "sonant allusion" deftly "nullifies these other terms for [human] height," leaving only YHWH high and exalted.[19]

This density of spatial rhetoric is unmatched in the book, with the sole exception of 5:15–16, which is semantically related to the present passage.[20]

> Humanity is bowed down, people are brought low,
> and the eyes of the high are brought low
> But YHWH of hosts is high in justice,
> and the holy God shows himself holy in righteousness. (5:15–16)[21]

---

19. Barré, "Rhetorical-Critical Study," 533.
20. On the relationship between 5:15–16 and ch. 2, see Moberly, "Whose Justice?" 64.
21. Translation from ibid., 56.

In Isa 2, we see no fewer than thirteen terms that describe the humiliation of humanity and the exaltation of YHWH in vv. 12–16. In addition, there appears to be a development in theme between each verse that frames vv. 12–16. Whereas v. 9 refers to the abasement of "humanity" and "man," vv. 11 and 17 refer to the abasement of humanity's "eyes" and "height." Verses 11 and 17 clarify the point that YHWH's opposition is not to humanity as such but, specifically, to human "loftiness." Other differences obtain, but the key remains that, whereas in v. 9 the prophet exhorts listeners not to "lift," or "elevate," humanity, vv. 11 and 17 concentrate on the elevation of YHWH. The coordination of שׁפל ("to be low") and שׁחח ("to be bowed down") in vv. 9, 11, and 17 anticipate the use of these terms throughout First Isaiah (21×).[22]

Verses 19–21 complete the downward plunge of all would-be opponents, as though they were not already trampled. Verses 20–21 are prose and may be an editorial expansion. The precipitating cause of the expansion in vv. 20–21 seems to be an interest in *enacting* the commands of vv. 10 and 19,[23] and thereby reinforcing the passage's juxtaposition of divine exaltation and human abasement.[24] As YHWH arises in terror and splendor, idol-makers consign their idols to the "rocky caves" and "dust," and their makers hide in "rocks" and "crevices in the crags." The scene corresponds in more frightening terms to Moses hiding in the rocky cave on Mount Sinai as YHWH passed in all his glory. The other similarity observed with this passage is the theophanic arrival of YHWH in Ps 29, which startles and disrupts the created world as YHWH roars with his powerful voice. In Ps 29, YHWH's coming also shatters the "cedars of Lebanon" (v. 6), but without the same focus on elevated features. To that extent, Isa 2 stands apart and above its literary parallels.[25]

Political Alliances and Idolatry (2:6–8)

The prophet's emphasis on demolishing *human* "loftiness" raises questions around the precise object of the polemic. Are we to interpret these terms in a purely moral sense, such that YHWH is opposed to human *pride*? Isaiah 2:6–22 provides us with a partially affirmative answer, but the passage also suggests a more complex picture, one that in First Isaiah certainly takes on a political hue.

---

22. Isa 5:15 and 29:4 also as a pair.
23. This is so especially if one reads ובאו in v. 19 as an original imperative, which is plausible though not definitive based on a comparison with v. 10. However, the LXX evidence argues against this suggestion. In any case, the subject of ובאו is ambiguous and may refer to the idolaters or the אלילים.
24. See similar juxtapositions in Isa 5:13–17. These verses suggest that Isaiah's focus on the אלילים is part of a larger "human exaltation" motif in these early chapters.
25. Cf. the grouping of Lebanon and Bashan in 33:9; Jer 22:20; Nah 1:4.

Humanity raises itself up (for a fall) insofar as it entrusts itself to false sources of power and, specifically, foreign alliances, a theme of immense significance in First Isaiah.[26] This seems to be where the whole passage, in its final form, ultimately leads (v. 22). Political alliances became associated with idolatry.[27] We will look first at how this occurs in the prophetic indictment (vv. 6–8) before turning toward other passages.

In vv. 6–8, the prophet announces that YHWH has forsaken his people. The causes of this abandonment emerge in a catalog of offenses. The prophet specifies divination, "grasping hands" with foreigners, excessive wealth, accumulation of horses and chariots, and fraudulent gods. What looks on first glance like a grab bag list reveals a certain logic on closer inspection. To begin, vv. 7–8 highlight two major *objects* of human trust, (1) wealth (silver, gold, storehouses) and (2) power (horses, chariots), and two primary *means* of seeking guidance or protection, namely, (1) divination and (2) idolatry (fraudulent gods, works of human hands). The specific objects within each category in the list appear to be representative and thus fitting for an indictment. The guiding rhetorical emphasis falls on the fact that Israel's land was "full" (4×; *מלא) of such contraband and illicit practices, such that there was "no end" (2×) to them. The image of fullness contrasts sharply with Isaiah's vision in ch. 6, where the whole land was—or would become—"full" of YHWH's glory. All that filled Israel's land was contrary to God's purposes for Israel and lulled her into a false sense of security.

Roberts suggests that the objects in 2:6–8 pertain to the Syro-Ephraimite crisis. For instance, "soothsayers"—or "intermediaries between the divine and human realms" (v. 6; cf. Deut 18:10–14)—were elsewhere described as "giving support to political decisions (Jer 27:9), and they are probably mentioned here because of their support for the Aramean-Israelite coalition against Judah." The great numbers of horses and chariots in v. 7 "suggests mobilization for war."[28] While Roberts's insistence that the Syro-Ephraimite crisis forms the specific backdrop to this passage may overspecify the evidence, the objects included in vv. 6–8 fit the prophet's broader critique of political alliance and military self-sufficiency. They may have been rooted in the Syro-Ephraimite crisis and then dehistoricized to allow for the prophet's more sweeping critique.

Of the items listed in 2:6–8, only the *idols* retain the prophet's attention through the rest of the chapter. The prophet returns to them in vv. 18 and 20. This narrowed focus could be explained on redactional grounds, namely, that vv. 6–7 and 12–16 were the original core of the passage and that vv. 8, 18, and

---

26. Isa 20:5; 30:5, 7; 31:1–3.
27. Brekelmans, "Deuteronomistic Influence in Isaiah 1–12," 169, refers to the "various texts against all human pride . . . [and] the sayings against all trust in alliances and treaties" as distinctive contributions of First Isaiah
28. Roberts, *First Isaiah*, 45.

20 were later redactions that shift attention toward the sin of idolatry.[29] Blenkinsopp argues something similar but insists that v. 8a is the original core.[30] There is indeed no reason to doubt that at least the phrase "their land has been filled with fraudulent gods (אלילים)" (v. 8a) was part of the poem's earliest stratum. It fits squarely with the syntactic structure of the preceding verse (object + ותמלא ארצו).

One plausible explanation for the turn toward idolatry as the focal sin in v. 8b–c, and then in the rest of the passage (vv. 18, 20), is that the appearance of the term אלילים in v. 8a triggered an editorial gloss in v. 8b–c, which doubled as a summary of the objects and behaviors listed in vv. 6–7. I will return to this suggestion below, but note here that v. 8 lands the final series of gut punches in the form of a triplet:

> Their land has been filled with fraudulent gods;
> to the works of their hands they bow,
> to that which their fingers have made.

The strategy employed here, of using couplets (vv. 6–7) followed by an emphatic (final) triplet, is well-known in biblical poetry, as is the use of a lead-off couplet to mark the initial boundary of an oracle.[31] The prophetic judgment in vv. 12–16 begins with a triplet. But the key point here is that vv. 6–8 bring reliance on military strength, wealth, and idolatry into collocation but then conclude the climactic sequence with a focus on idolatry. The charge of idolatry is the capstone of the prophet's critique. Within this critique, idolatry is the underlying malaise driving Israel toward reliance on foreign powers and wealth.

Isaiah 31:1–3

The concurrence of the three objects of trust mentioned in Isa 2:6–8 (power, wealth, and idolatry) can be discerned elsewhere in the prophet's critiques. Judah's attempts to secure alliances with Egypt and Assyria are consistently reframed in "religious" terms.[32] The prophet utters a powerful threefold condemnation in Isa 31:1, for instance:

> Woe to those going down to Egypt for help!
>> They *depend* on <u>horses</u>.
>> They trust in <u>chariots</u>, for they are many!

---

29. See Williamson, "Productive Textual Error."
30. Blenkinsopp, *Isaiah 1–39*, 194.
31. Couey, *Reading the Poetry*, 96–100.
32. E.g., Isa 7:7–9; 22:8–11; 30:1–5; 31:1–3. Cf. Roberts, *First Isaiah*, 45–46.

And in <u>horsemen</u>, for they are numerous!
But they do not depend on the Holy One of Israel,
And do not seek YHWH.

Israel's reliance on Egyptian political and military strength was perceived as a betrayal of YHWH and a divinizing of military might. Because of their idolatrous nature, the prophet yielded no ground to political alliances. The editor of Isa 31 then strengthens the connection between the folly of military trust and idolatry in v. 7, when in a prose addition the writer anticipates a day of disillusionment that would coincide with the failure of military powers:

For on that day each person will reject his <u>fraudulent gods</u> (אלילים) of silver,
 and his <u>fraudulent gods</u> (אלילים) of gold,
which your sinful hands made for you.

The failure of Egypt will lead, ultimately, to the rejection of the אלילים (v. 7) and, in the same breath, to the destruction of the Assyrians (v. 8). Spatial language plays a role here. Just as Egyptian aid would "stumble ... and fall (*נפל*)," YHWH brings about the "fall" (*נפל*) of Assyria (v. 8). Idolatrous alliances would be utterly abased before the God who "rises" (*רום*) against wicked nations (v. 3).

Roberts insists that the focus on idolatry in v. 7 also fits with the prophet's overarching concern to undermine Israel (and Judah's) trust in military alliances formed through consultation of deities. Consulting deities before battle would have been commonplace, and troops were known to bring small figurines into battle for consultation and protection (cf. 2 Sam 5:17–21). Isaiah 31 may have its specific origin in the military aid that an anti-Assyrian contingent from Judah sought to obtain from Egypt during the period 705–700. The prophet considered this a dead-end endeavor or worse. In fact, the military aid never came through.[33] Whether the consulted idols envisioned here are Yahwistic or not, the author, "with a Jerusalemite perspective, dismisses them as the work of human hands" (31:7).[34]

The use of אל in 31:3 is interesting in First Isaiah, especially in light of the prophet's general preference for אלילים. Isaiah writes that "the Egyptians are human, and not divine" (מצרים אדם ולא אל). Wildberger suggests that the prophet avoided using the term אלהים, "since one would immediately think of Yahweh."[35] The term אל does occur on two other occasions in First Isaiah. It occurs once in

---

33. Hanson, *Political History*, 263
34. Roberts, *First Isaiah*, 46.
35. Wildberger, *Isaiah 28–35*, 213.

reference to the sign-child עמנואל in 7:14 and in reference to YHWH himself (as אל גבור) in 9:5.³⁶ The application to human aid as לא אל and לא רוח reflects the prophet's concern to disabuse Israel of the idea that Egypt or any other nation constituted a viable object of trust. In Isa 31:8 the prophet uses the phrase לא־איש to speak of the sword that YHWH would use to bring down Assyria. The point there is that Assyria's downfall would *not* come by means of the לא אל Egypt. Only in YHWH could protection be found.

Isaiah 30:1–5 picks up many of the same themes. The prophet insists that Judah must not seek "protection" or "shelter" from Egypt, for these would only result in "shame" and "humiliation" (vv. 2–3). In the adjoining oracle, the prophet portrays the countless envoys of "treasures" going down to Egypt on the backs of donkeys and camels. These envoys were undoubtedly tribute payments for Egyptian military aid. As a point of connection to our focus text, the same term for "treasures" (אצרות) used here in 30:6 appears also in 2:7, in the prophet's accusation, which also includes references to horses and chariots. This would lead one to infer that something like the circumstances outlined in Isa 30–31 were in view in Isa 2. Judah depended on riches to buy Egyptian protection but failed to trust in YHWH.

Other passages in First Isaiah voice similar warnings. Judah sought its own alliances and defenses without due regard for YHWH. Consider the following:

> He has removed the covering of Judah. But in that day *you looked* (*נבט) to the weaponry of the Forest House. And the breeches in the City of David *you considered* (*ראה)—for there were many!—and you stored up water in the lower pool. And the houses of Jerusalem you counted, and you pulled down the houses to fortify the wall (לבצר החומה). And you made a reservoir between the walls for the waters of the old pool, but you *did not look* (*נבט) to the one who made it, and its creator from long ago you *did not consider* (*ראה; 22:8–11).

---

36. Goldingay, "Compound Name in Isaiah 9:5(6)." Goldingay argues convincingly that the phrase אל גבור refers to YHWH, and not the king (cf. Isa 10:21, where the same phrase is used in clear reference to YHWH). It is indeed a name for the child but describes YHWH. Goldingay points, for example, to the human name עמנו אל in Isa 7:14, which also describes God. Moreover, the other names in Isa 9:5 refer in other places to YHWH himself, and the appellative אביעד ("eternal father") is unprecedented in reference to a king. Goldingay renders the nominal clauses in 9:5(6) as follows: "One who plans a wonder is the warrior God; the father forever is a commander who brings peace." (p. 243). His following comments make the point: "The opening designation of YHWH as planner and his uninstanced designation as commander at the end are predicates which have implicitly theological and metaphorical significance. They declare that YHWH is a certain sort of planner and commander—specifically, one who is better than Tiglath-pileser (*pl'sr*, Akkadian *šarru rābû?*)" (p. 243).

Here again, the prophet lambasts Judah for depending on its own strength to protect against an imminent Assyrian attack. Some surmise that the fall of Babylon to Assyria forms the backdrop for the present oracle.[37] Without their ally, Judah was now fully exposed. But rather than turning to YHWH, they "looked to the weaponry of the Forest House" (v. 8), a pathetic attempt at gaining security with an approaching Assyrian army. The twofold repetition of *נבט ("to look") and *ראה ("to see/regard") at the beginning and end of the section reinforces the prophet's concerns over political dependence. Such dependence stood at odds with dependence on, and regard for, YHWH. The reader might also note that Isaiah considers such defensive moves futile (2:12–16). For although Judah made plans "to fortify the wall" (לבצר החומה; 22:8, 10) YHWH was coming "against every fortified wall" (על־חומה בצורה; 2:15).[38]

The means and objects of trust in Isa 2—divination and idolatry, wealth and power—ultimately prove destructive to their devotees. Because they "bow down," they are abased (3×) and brought low (3×). YHWH is simultaneously exalted (lit., "up high"). In other words, YHWH's exaltation correlates with the moment when false sources of power, whether human or allegedly divine, are revealed as useless frauds. This is why the derisive term אלילים plays such a key role in ch. 2. It highlights the vacuous nature of other so-called "gods," their sudden vaporization, and the pure folly of holding them in regard. The term rightly captures that moment when the alleged אלהים are exposed as worthless.

The אלילים in Isaiah 2

The אלילים receive mention three times in Isa 2 (vv. 8, 18, 20), and the chapter focuses on illicit cultic activity on two other occasions (vv. 6, 22). In other words, *denouncements* of the cult go together with *pronouncements* concerning YHWH's exclusive exaltation. But more to the point, it is *humanity*'s attempted self-exaltation (vv. 8–9, 11, 17–18, 20–22) through image-making that the prophet exposes. Image-making is, according to the prophet, a form of abasement—but it is only exposed as such in "that day" when YHWH comes against every raised thing:

> The haughtiness of humanity will be brought down,
> and the stature of men will be made low.
> YHWH *alone* will be exalted in that day,
> and the fraudulent gods [אלילים] will pass away. (Isa 2:17–18)

---

37. Roberts, *First Isaiah*, 288.
38. Notice that 22:8 refers to "in that day" (ביום ההוא) and 2:12 to the fact that "YHWH has a day" (יום ליהוה).

In Isa 2, the prophet is obviously not mocking fraud *gods* as such, for they are non-divinities. There is no divine being to ridicule. Instead, they denounce the אלילים-*makers*, who are the true frauds behind the gods, just as the prophets were the con artists behind the אליל they espoused.[39] Notice the emphasis on *making* idols in vv. 8 and 20:

> Their land has been filled with fraudulent gods (אלילים);
> to *the works of their hands* they bow, [idolatry]
> to *that which their fingers have made*. . . .
> In that day humanity will cast to the moles and bats
> the fraudulent gods of silver and the fraudulent gods (אלילים) of gold,
> *which they made for themselves to worship* (vv. 8, 20)

Like other idol polemics, these verses draw out the folly of worshiping one's own creation. Confronted with YHWH's supremacy, the idol makers toss their objects to the shrews and bats in caves and among rocks. The shrews, likely the type mummified by Egyptians and deemed sacred, are here already in the underworld.[40] The bats are unclean animals according to Deut 14:18 and Lev 11:19. Thus, the prophet, like Ezekiel, envisions the ultimate demotion of images from revered to defiled, and ultimately, the exposure of the idol makers as frauds.

The chapter thus nears its end with YHWH exalted and humanity and images defiled. It then reaches its climax in v. 22, with the prophet's exhortation:

> Quit your (obsession) with humans (האדם),
> in whose nostrils is breath (נשמה).
> For why should he be considered (*חשב)?

With this final query, readers may recall the psalmist's analogous reflection:

> What are humans, that you should call them to mind,
> or mortals, that you attend to them? (Ps 8:4)

The primary difference, of course, is that in this latter text, it is YHWH who regards the human, and the human who marvels that YHWH should do so. The psalmist goes on to proclaim the astonishing glory and stature that crowns humans. Indeed "all things" are under their feet, as they sit and rule over creation. First Isaiah, by contrast, sees little reason on this occasion to celebrate

---

39. For an alternative proposal, which is not wholly incompatible with the one offered here, see Hays, "What Sort of Friends?"

40. *HALOT*, ad loc. The Hebrew phrase לחפר פרות is rendered לחפרפרים ("to the shrews") in 1QIsaᵃ.

the exalted status of humanity and marvels instead at the astonishing exaltation of YHWH. Where the psalmist declares the "majesty" (הדר, 8:5) of humanity, set above all things, Isaiah declares the "majesty" (הדר; 2:19, 21) of YHWH, above all else, and in clear opposition to any human that would lift themself up. The elevation of humankind in the face of divine majesty is sheer folly.

Isaiah's final words in v. 22 find an even closer analogy in the words of another psalmist. In Ps 144, the poet asks:

> Oh YHWH, what are humans,
> that you acknowledge them?
> Mortals (בן אנוש), that you regard (*חשב) them?
> Humans are like vapor,
> Their days pass like a shadow. (vv. 3–4)

This psalmist also marvels that God would give such attention to mortals, given their ephemerality. They are הבל (v. 4). But the mere fact that humans are "vapor," and with days "like a shadow," gives Isaiah reason to pause. It is one thing for a human to marvel that God should regard humankind but quite another for humans to regard one another with the reverence due God. The prophet thus returns to a plural cohortative, as in Isa 2:5, and urges Israel to "stop trusting in humans." Since images lack power, then devotion to the אלילים is really trust in humans, their creators, who are utterly abased before the exalted God. In the spatial logic of First Isaiah, only what is utterly exalted is worthy of worship. In this way, Isaiah brings his initial judgment to its climax by dissolving the human as a viable object of ultimate trust. If the gods have disappeared into cracks in the ground, and their makers exposed, then depending on flesh and breath is absurd.

Not surprisingly, then, the word אלילים occurs in later contexts that draw attention to their human origins. To highlight an example from the Holiness Code, YHWH urges the people: "Do not turn to האלילים, and do not make for yourselves molten gods; I am YHWH your God" (Lev 19:4). The use of the definite article suggests a known phenomenon, like "the Asherim," though we have no clear indication from the use of אלילים in the Hebrew Bible that the term has a referent that would differentiate substantially from other terms for idols.[41] Here in Lev 19:4, the אלילים are likened to molten gods that the people make "for themselves." Leviticus 26:1 also emphasizes the human-made nature of these non-deities in a trifold arrangement:

> Do not make yourselves אלילם;

---

41. Cf. Ps 97:7; Isa 2:18; 19:3.

do not erect a molten image for yourselves;
and do not place a carved stone in your land to bow down and worship it,
    for I am YHWH your God.

This text develops the point made in Lev 19:4. The phrase "Do not make yourselves אלילם" follows the same exact syntactical and semantic pattern used elsewhere in the phrase "You shall not make yourselves" + אלהים or "You shall not make yourselves" + פסלים. This pattern derives, of course, from the Torah and its cultic prohibition on making images or gods. The object is typically אלהים:

You shall not make yourself an <u>image</u>, or anything like that which is in the skies above, or on the earth below, or in the waters beneath the earth. (Exod 20:4)	לא תעשה־לך פסל וכל־תמונה אשר בשמים ממעל ואשר בארץ מתחת ואשר במים מתחת לארץ
You shall not make <u>gods</u> of silver alongside me. And <u>gods</u> of gold *you shall not make for yourselves*. (Exod 20:23)	לא תעשון אתי אלהי כסף ואלהי זהב לא תעשו לכם
You shall not make yourself any cast <u>gods</u>. (Exod 34:17)	אלהי מסכה לא תעשה־לך
You shall not make yourself an <u>image</u>, or anything like that which is in the skies above, or on the earth below, or in the waters beneath the earth. (Deut 5:8)	לא תעשה־לך פסל וכל־תמונה אשר בשמים ממעל ואשר בארץ מתחת ואשר במים מתחת לארץ
Do not turn aside to <u>hand-crafted gods</u>. Cast <u>gods</u> *you shall not make for yourselves*. I am YHWH your God. (Lev 19:4)	אל־תפנו אל־האלילים ואלהי מסכה לא תעשו לכם אני יהוה אלהיכם
You shall not make for yourselves <u>hand-crafted gods</u>. (Lev 26:1)	לא־תעשו לכם אלילם

Texts such as Lev 19:4 and 26:1 freely replace אלהים with אלילים. The pattern above suggests a consistent association with handcraftedness. Earlier texts such as Exod 20:23 and 34:16 do not send any clear signals that handcraftedness negates the possibility of divinity. Indeed, idol makers in the ancient Near East had specific rituals to deny that idol makers crafted deities. There was indeed a ritual moment when an idol became a deity.[42] However, as is well known from Deutero-Isaiah, the handmade origins of other nations' deities became a source of mockery and derision.[43] The focus of such texts was to expose the idol makers as frauds. In this sense, the polemics of Deutero-Isaiah are more accurately

---

42. Dick, *Born in Heaven*; Walker and Dick, *Induction of the Cult Image*.
43. Smith, "Polemic of Biblical Monotheism," 201–34.

referred to as idol-maker polemics.⁴⁴ This lends similarity between the prophetic critiques in First Isaiah and the idol-maker polemics in Second Isaiah.

However, there are also differences. While I will make a case that the term is derisive, the absence of any sustained ridicule in these texts sets the term apart from the kind of idol *polemics* we see in Deutero-Isaiah. Instead, First Isaiah deploys the term אלילים in judgment oracles. YHWH is judging Israel for its attachment to אלילים, or "frauds" (broadly construed), and prophesying a day when they would toss their אלילים into limestone cracks and crevasses, into the underworld itself where they properly belong.

The Relationship Between Isaiah 2:6–22 and Other Anti-Idol Texts in the Hebrew Bible

Possible Deutero-Isaian Affinities

While most scholars find a preexilic core in Isa 2:6–22*, many argue that the passage's anti-image language (or anti-image-maker language) derives from a late exilic or postexilic context linked literarily to the Deuteronomistic History or Deutero-Isaiah.⁴⁵ Wildberger suggests that 2:10ff belong to an exilic or early postexilic redaction because of the emphasis on YHWH's sole exaltation and the critique of idols.⁴⁶ Cazales attributes the reference to wealth in v. 7a, idol worship in v. 8b, the humiliation of humanity in v. 9a, and the entirety of vv. 20–21 to Deutero-Isaiah.⁴⁷ Blenkinsopp argues that the description of the אלילים in v. 8b is "one of the most obvious additions to this poetic core." The phrases, "to the work of their hands they bow down, to that which their fingers have made," according to Blenkinsopp, are standard fare "anti-idolatry polemic of a kind frequently encountered in the second part of the book . . . , [and are] probably therefore from the late Neo-Babylonian or early Persian period."⁴⁸ Blenkinsopp does not discuss the uniqueness of the phrase (אשר עשו אצבעתיו, "that which their fingers have made"), which occurs here and in Isa 17:8 and nowhere else in the Hebrew Bible (cf. Ps 8:4). Becker labels vv. 8, 19,

---

44. See Smith, "Polemic of Biblical Monotheism"; MacDonald, "Monotheism and Isaiah," 46.
45. See examples listed in Brekelmans, "Deuteronomistic Influence," 167–76. For Berges, *Das Buch Jesaja*, 79, on the other hand, the references to אלילים are manifestly postexilic, linked to the nations' journey to Zion as they were in Pss 96–97.
46. Wildberger, *Isaiah 28–39*, 547.
47. Cazelles, "Qui aurait visé?" 420
48. Blenkinsopp, *Isaiah 1–39*, 194.

20–21 "götzenpolemische Nachinterpretation" after the style of Deutero-Isaiah.⁴⁹ After denying Deuteronomic influence, Brekelmans asserts that First Isaiah's depiction of fraudulent gods (אלילים) made by hands "seems . . . more in line with Deutero-Isaiah," and with Clements argues that "the implicit rejection of the religious use of images because they are made by human hands must presuppose the anti-idolatry polemic of Is 44,9–20."⁵⁰

While a *thematic* emphasis on critiquing image makers bears a certain affinity to Deutero-Isaiah, First Isaiah's lexical distinctiveness suggests otherwise. The chart in appendix 1 demonstrates the fundamental differences between the terms that First Isaiah uses for illicit objects of cultic devotion and language for similar objects in Deutero-Isaiah. The contrast is stark. Moreover, the general syntax and diction in First Isaiah is sufficiently different from Deutero-Isaiah to render doubtful a set of direct editorial insertions.⁵¹ In his 2006 commentary on Isa 1–5, Williamson argues that, while the term אלילים is early, the anti-idol texts in vv. 8b, 18 are redactional insertions, most likely deriving (along with v. 6 "house of Jacob," and vv. 8b–9, and 18) from a redactor contemporaneous with Deutero-Isaiah when concerns about idolatry find their "greatest concentration."⁵² He even floats the possibility that it was Deutero-Isaiah who added the anti-idol texts. However, in a 2015 publication, Williamson changed his view in light of further consideration of the major differences between the depiction of idols in Isa 1–39 and 40–48.⁵³ Whereas Isa 1–39 addresses idolatry "within Yahwistic religion," Isa 40–48 confronts Babylonian idols.⁵⁴ Moreover, there are significant terminological differences, some of which I also note in appendix 1.⁵⁵ Williamson then concludes that the anti-idol texts must, for the

---

49. Becker, *Jesaja*, 170. Becker also considers vv. 2:6aα, 7, 9, 11, 19 historicizing redactions, which insist that the day of YHWH is already at hand *in contrast to* the eschatologically oriented core in vv. 12–17 (p. 171); see also Kratz, *Kyros im Deuterojesaja-Buch*, 201ff. A. 652–63.

50. Ibid., 172, citing Clements, 44.

51. E.g., Isa 2:8 refers to אשר עשו אצבעתיו, a phrase which never occurs in DH. At the most, we might speak of First Isaiah's radical extension and development of a brief phrase that occurs frequently, but not exclusively, in Deuteronomistic literature (i.e., מעשה־ידים). See the use of this phrase in reference to human-crafted images in Deut 4:28; 27:15; 31:29; 2 Kgs 19:18 (// Isa 37:19); 22:17; Ps 115:4; 135:15; Isa 17:8; Jer 10:3; 25:6, 7 (possibly v. 14); 32:30 (?); Hos 14:3; Mic 5:12; 2 Chr 32:19. There is one enigmatic reference to מעשיך, either "your deeds" or "your works [i.e., images]" in Trito-Isaiah (57:12). The next section discusses this possibility.

52. Williamson, *Critical and Exegetical Commentary*, 1:211–12. Williamson assigns vv. 20–22 to a yet later date. Williamson also argues in the same context that the phrase "work of their hands" in 2:8 is Deuteronomistic. While Isaiah may have penned these words, they fit "more comfortably" in a later period (1:212).

53. Williamson, "Idols in Isaiah," 22–23. I had come to a similar conclusion in a 2013 paper on the subject (Lynch, "First Isaiah").

54. Williamson, "Idols in Isaiah," 26.

55. Ibid., 23.

most part, date to a period "considerably later" than Deutero-Isaiah.⁵⁶ While I am less committed to dating First Isaiah's anti-idol texts to the postexilic period, I agree with his conclusion that the anti-idol rhetoric in Isa 1–39 is distinct.

The next issue to consider, then, is the degree to which the anti-image-maker texts in First Isaiah aligns with Deuteronomistic and other biblical phraseology.⁵⁷

Possible Deuteronomistic Affinities

If the anti-idolatry texts in Isa 2 are not Deutero-Isaian interpolations, one might be tempted to attribute them to Deuteronomistic influence. Some, such as Vermeylen, Kaiser, Williamson, and Kilian, argue for a Deuteronomistic redaction or influence on the anti-idol language in First Isaiah.⁵⁸ For Kaiser and Kilian, the polemics against idolatry betray Deuteronomistic influence.⁵⁹ The strongest link with Deuteronomic language is the phrase "works of . . . hands." For instance, "They bow down to *the work of their hands*, to what their own fingers have made" (Isa 2:8), which is roughly parallel to the claim in Deut 4:28 that "they will serve gods *made by human hands*," and the prohibition on making a molten image, "*the work of human hands*" in Deut 27:15.⁶⁰ Similar language, obviously Deuteronomistic, occurs in 2 Kgs 19:18 // Isa 37:19, and in other texts in the book of Jeremiah.⁶¹ In addition, the term פסיל, found several times in First Isaiah, also occurs with some frequency in the Deuteronomistic History.⁶²

As suggested in the introduction, the idea of Deutero-Isaian or Deuteronomistic insertions often hinge on an evolutionary view of monotheism's development wherein First Isaiah *could not* possibly be the progenitor of anti-idolatry language, or even a distinctive creative voice on the subject. Brekelmans insists that "everyone agrees that the way of speaking about gods in the Old Testament period shows a certain development." A "real derision" of other deities emerges in Jeremiah and Deutero-Isaiah, and thus the derisive speech about other deities in First Isaiah belongs to the same period.⁶³ I suggest that we are best advised

---

56. Ibid., 25. Williamson also discusses this redactional layer in "Productive Textual Error."

57. Cf. the relationship between Mic 5:9–13 and Isa 2:6–8. It is worth noting that Isa 2:2–4 draws from Mic 4, and then 2:6ff from Mic 5.

58. Williamson, *Isaiah 1–5*, 212; following Hoffmann, *Die Intention der Verkündigung Jesajas*; Brekelmans, "Deuteronomic Influence," 169; Beuken, *Jesaja 1–12*, 101. Beuken is more modest in his claims, stating that, e.g., vv. 19–21 "erinnert an das deuteronomistische Motiv der Abschwörung fremder Götter, wobei das verwendete Vokabular für eine sicherer Datierung aber zu begrenzt ist. Die Verse passen in die Zeit sowohl vor als auch nach dem Exil."

59. Killian, *Jesaja II. 13–39*, 31, cited in Brekelmans, "Deuteronomic Influence," 171.

60. Brekelmans, "Deuteronomic Influence," 171.

61. Cf. also 2 Kgs 17 and references in Jeremiah.

62. Isa 10:10; 21:9; 30:22; cf. Deut 7:5, 25; 12:3; Judg 3:19, 26; 2 Kgs 17:41.

63. Brekelmans, "Deuteronomic Influence," 171.

to avoid this imposition of religious-historical assumptions onto First Isaiah. Nevertheless, we are left with the possibility of family resemblance wherein First Isaiah may have shared certain phrases with the Deuteronomistic Historian *and other biblical traditions* but inflected them to such a degree that rendering their source with any certainty is nearly impossible.

As a case study in Deuteronomistic influence, let us look at vv. 8 and 20 in more detail:

ותמלא ארצו אלילים
למעשה ידיו ישתחוו
לאשר עשו אצבעתיו

Their land has been filled with fraudulent gods;
to the works of their hands they bow,
to that which their fingers have made. (2:8)

The first poetic line is unique to First Isaiah. The second uses the מעשה + ידים phrase used on occasion in Deuteronomic/Deuteronomistic literature in reference to idols (e.g., Deut 4:28; 27:15; 2 Kgs 19:18). Psalms 115:4 and 135:15 also refer to idols using the same construction. However, the phrasing is not inherently tied to idolatry. Secular uses of the phrase appear in Song 7:2, in reference to the jewels of a master artist (applied here to the thighs of the man's lover). Elsewhere, the phrase מעשה + ידים refers to YHWH's own creations. Isaiah 29:23 describes Jacob's children as "the work of my [YHWH's] hands" (מעשה ידי). Similarly, Isa 60:21 refers to the people of God planted in the land as "the work of my hands" (מעשה ידי). Lamentations 4:2 compares Zion to "earthen pots, the work of a potter's hands" (מעשה ידי יוצר).

The frequency and range of use of the phrases above cast into serious doubt any attempt to link this verse definitively to Deuteronomistic influence. The construction in the final poetic line—אצבעת + *עשׂה—never appears in Deuteronomistic literature. Instead, it appears only in connection with YHWH's creative acts in Ps 8:4: "When I gaze upon your heavens, the works of your fingers (מעשה אצבעתיך), the moon and the stars that you fixed in place." Similarly, the final verse of Isa 2 (v. 22) bears a striking similarity with Ps 8:5, though with a decidedly different point. Humans are unworthy of regard when they rob YHWH of his due. The precise extent of the links between Isa 2 and Ps 8 are uncertain, but these two open up the possibility that the phrase מעשה + ידים might have also derived from Psalms (115:4 and 135:15) and not, in the first place, from Deuteronomistic literature.

As a second case study in Deuteronomistic influence, we move now to consider Isa 2:20, a text about which I suggest we can be more optimistic about Deuteronomistic influence. This claim, however, rests on another more problematic set of assumptions about such influence in the book of Exodus. In the end, we may be better placed simply to suggest influence from Exodus. Two phrases from Isa 2:20 deserve special attention:

ביום ההוא ישליך האדם את אלילי כספו ואת אלילי זהבו
אשר עשו־לו להשתחות לחפר פרות ולעטלפים

In that day humanity will cast to the moles and bats their fraudulent <u>gods of silver and their fraudulent gods of gold</u>, <u>which they made for themselves to worship</u>

The phrase "their fraudulent gods of silver and their fraudulent gods of gold, which they made for themselves" finds resonance across Deuteronomic and Deuteronomistic literature. Deuteronomy 7:25 refers to the gold overlay on gods. Deutero-Isaiah also describes the costly materials used to cover images (40:19; 46:6). The closest similarities exist between Isa 2:20 and Exod 20:23, which uses the more closely related phrase, לא תעשו אתי אלהי כסף ואלהי זהב לא תעשו לכם, "You shall not make alongside me gods of silver, and gods of gold you shall not make for yourselves." Noticeably, Isa 2:20 seems to substitute אלילים for the אלהים used in its more well-known counterpart:

אלהי כסף ואלהי זהב לא תעשו לכם (Exod 20:23)
אלילי כספו ואת אלילי זהבו אשר עשו־לו (Isa 2:20)

The similarities between these texts are so striking that literary dependence on Exod 20:23 seems likely. Yet as I discuss below, that dependency may be by way of Isa 31:7. The substitution of אלילים for אלהים heightens the rhetorical point that the glinting gold and silver objects have no divine status and, despite their material value, are only worthy of casting to the moles and bats in underground caves. The lexical substitution of אלילים for the gods denies images the dignity of the term אלהים, as if such language would be inappropriate in the same breath as one referred to the defiled images. Only the אלהי יעקב is worthy of divinity (Isa 2:3).

The substitution is similar to Ezekiel's refusal to use the term אלהים, as noted by Kutsko. Ezekiel replaces the Deuteronomic phrase עבד אלהים . . . עץ ואבן "to serve gods . . . of wood and stone" (Deut 4:28; 28:36; 28:64) with שרת עץ ואבן "to worship wood and stone" (Ezek 20:32).[64] Kutsko observes that, while Deuteronomy (and Deutero-Isaiah) "disparage idolatry, Ezekiel is downright blunt about it: devotees of idols do not worship wood and stone gods; they worship mere wood and stone."[65] Kutsko points out that the notion of substitution

---

64. Kutsko, *Between Heaven and Earth*, 39.
65. Ibid., 40.

is not an argument from silence but rather a "deliberate strategy." In addition to the example above, Ezekiel also substitutes the term גלולים for אלהים on several occasions.⁶⁶ The use of a defiling term in Ezekiel bears striking similarities to the defiling association with "bats," in Isa 2:20 (cf. Lev 11:19; Deut 14:18). Both prophets insist that idols defile and thus belong with defiling animals.

In sum, Isa 2:8 and 20 bear similarities to Deuteronomistic texts, though significant differences also exist. To claim that these verses are Deuteronomistic *interpolations*, however, creates more problems than it solves and does not account for the unique variations on common anti-idol ideas that exist across the biblical literature. A theory of direct interpolation—or even influence—leaves too many portions of these verses unexplained. The strongest similarity exists between Isa 2:20 and Exod 20:23, a text of debated Deuteronomistic relation, but even this text is not appropriated without a striking lexical substitution.

But we might pause here to ask what is at stake in determining whether or not the anti-idolatry verses in Isa 2 are indigenous or derivative. Perhaps the primary issue is whether, or the degree to which, we consider anti-idolatry texts part of First Isaiah's own voice, or contribution, to the canonical conversation about YHWH's superiority. Those who attribute Isa 2:8 and 20 to other hands typically do so on the assumption that (a) the concern with idolatry derives from later periods in Israel's history and from other more obviously polemical voices, and (b) that monotheistic discourse matures in later texts. Whether or not Isa 2:8 and 20 are early or late, I submit that the study above demonstrates that their relationship to Deutero-Isaiah and Deuteronomistic literature is less significant than many suggest. First Isaiah, even if drawing from either of the latter, puts its own very distinct spin on the concepts inherited. Influence may have even flowed in the other direction.⁶⁷ The distinct contribution of First Isaiah comes by way of linking its derision of other deities to the prophetic call to abandon trust in foreign powers. Simultaneously, the prophet calls Israel to embrace its vision of YHWH, "lofty and exalted" (6:1), and against all powers that raise themselves up.

A Conversation Within First Isaiah

As mentioned above, the dependence of Isa 2:20 on Exod 20:23 may have been by way of Isa 31:7, or perhaps vice versa. In a very similar fashion, Isa 17:8 is clearly from the same literary hand as Isa 2:8:

---

66. Ibid., 36 (table 2).
67. Williamson, *Isaiah 1–5*, 217, seems to assume a development of First Isaiah's anti-idolatry themes through to Second Isaiah, though he does not account for the striking lexical differences (see appendix 1, p. 107).

ותמלא ארצו אלילים לְמַעֲשֵׂה ידיו ישתחוו לאשר עשו אצבעתיו (2:8)
ולא ישעה אל־המזבחות מַעֲשֵׂה ידיו ואשר עשו אצבעתיו לא יראה (17:8)
והאשרים והחמנים

בַּיּוֹם הַהוּא יַשְׁלִיךְ הָאָדָם אֵת אֱלִילֵי כַסְפּוֹ וְאֵת אֱלִילֵי זְהָבוֹ אֲשֶׁר עָשׂוּ־לוֹ (2:20)
להשתחות לחפר פרות ולעטלפים
כִּי בַיּוֹם הַהוּא יִמְאָסוּן אִישׁ אֱלִילֵי כַסְפּוֹ וֶאֱלִילֵי זְהָבוֹ אֲשֶׁר עָשׂוּ לָכֶם יְדֵיכֶם חֵטְא (31:7)

There are clear indications that, while on the one hand there may be some influence between First Isaiah and other anti-image texts in the Hebrew Bible, First Isaiah has its own way of speaking against images—for instance, using the phrase "that which their *fingers* have made" (Isa 2:8; 17:8) and substituting אלילים for אלהים. The very use of the term אלילים suggests that the prophet modified whatever anti-image language he may have inherited. Some of the borrowing and adaptation in Isa 2 seems to have occurred within the book of First Isaiah itself. For example, Isa 2:8 and 2:20 either draw from or are the basis of other texts in First Isaiah. What is crucial to note here is the formation of a distinct language around the non-divinity of handmade images.

The anti-idol language in 2:8 and 2:20 is thus closely aligned with 17:8 and 31:7, respectively. In conjunction with other semantic correspondences noted in the parallels above, it is reasonable to speak of Isa 2 drawing together themes from other oracles in chs. 1–35. It is likely that Isa 2 pulls from the few anti-idol sentiments present in other First Isaian texts, and fronts the entire literary corpus of First Isaiah, or whatever form he had, with an anti-idol theme.[68] This lends the otherwise political railings of the prophet a distinctive anti-idolatry flavor. Political alliances were reframed in terms of idolatry. Simultaneously, Isa 2 drew anti-idolatry rhetoric into close association with divine incomparability rhetoric, a move that neither 17:8 nor 31:7 made.[69]

---

68. See Williamson, "Productive Textual Error."
69. For Williamson, these anti-idolatry texts scattered throughout First Isaiah do not stand alone. They form part of a larger set of additions to First Isaiah. He writes:

> Five short anti-idol additions within the text of Isaiah 1–39 is certainly noteworthy, and so far as I am aware previous commentators have never thought of considering them together as a whole. Noting the similarities between them, however, inevitably leads us on with fresh urgency to ask what their significance might be. (Williamson, "Idols in Isaiah," 21)

Williamson then argues that they belong to a unified redactional layer. My study of the אלילים passages has come to a similar conclusion independently of Williamson but would be less optimistic about our ability to date them. Moreover, some texts such as 2:8 and 10:10–11 may be part of the book's earliest strata. Williamson dates all occurrences of the term after Isa 40–48, in the postexilic period (Williamson, "Idols in Isaiah," 24–25).

Before moving too quickly past these important intertexts, it is worth noting several of their key features. I will address Isa 10:10–11 and 19:1–3 in subsequent chapters but focus here on 17:8 and 31:7.[70]

Isaiah 17:7–8 form part of a set of loosely related prophetic in oracles 17:1–11. Verses 7–8 and 9–11 each begin with an "in that day" (ביום ההוא) oracle that expand beyond the initial focus on Damascus and Israel in vv. 1–6 and address "humanity" (אדם) as such. Verses 7–8 can be translated as follows:

In that day humanity will gaze upon their maker,
their eyes will look to the holy one of Israel.
And they will not gaze upon their altars, the work of their hands,
neither will they look to what their fingers have made, the asherim or incense stands.

These verses form a tight unity, bound by the repetition of "gaze" (*שעה) and "look" (*ראה) in vv. 7–8. Regarding YHWH, the creator, involves a decisive turn from the illicit cultic objects that one creates.[71] Wildberger notes that the critique of these cultic creations "is roughly the same as what one finds in the secondary additions to Deutero-Isaiah."[72] The emphasis on YHWH as creator, another prominent Deutero-Isaian theme, suggests this further. However, it is worth noting the total absence of any reference to gods or even images. Moreover, Deutero-Isaiah does not mention altars, incense stands, or asherim. Instead, Proto-Isaiah mentions altars and other cultic elements in ways that suggest that they were either proxies for talking about idols (notice the language of "work of their hands") or objects of critique on their own (17:7–8; 29:7; 30:22).

Isaiah 31:7 also follows an "in that day" (ביום ההוא) oracle that stretches from vv. 4–9, and with v. 6 is widely deemed to be redactional.[73] The passage foretells Zion's dramatic deliverance, when YHWH would come like a powerful bird and rescue Judah from the oppressing Assyrians. The oracle follows an oracle in vv. 1–3 in which the prophet excoriates the Israelites for seeking help from Egypt. In that oracle, the prophet urges Israel to rid themselves of any dependence on Egyptian military support, which they had apparently divinized (31:3). Though lacking specific semantic links, the deliverance oracle in vv. 4–9 suggests that the people would ultimately do so. They reject their אלילים (v. 7) in

---

70. I also address 31:7, briefly, in ch. 3.
71. Hans Wildberger, *Isaiah 13–27*, 175. The emphasis on humanity (האדם), and not specifically Israel or the nations, connects the passage back to the similar uses of האדם in Isa 2:17, 20, and 22.
72. Ibid., 179.
73. Berges, *Das Buch Jesaja*, 240; Childs, *Isaiah*, 231; Williamson, "Idols in Isaiah," 21; Beuken, *Jesaja*, 216; Wildberger, *Isaiah 28–39*, 219–20.

whom they trusted.[74] The close proximity of divinized אדם (v. 3) and the אלילים (v. 7) may form the basis for the last verse of Isa 2, where the prophet tells the people to stop trusting אדם (v. 22; after saying that they would dispose of their אלילים). Direction of influence is hard to determine, but it is at least worth noting here that Isa 2 anticipates many of the other uses of אלילים in First Isaiah.

A Conversation Between First Isaiah and Micah

In addition to affiliations within First Isaiah itself, we can also step back to observe several affinities between First Isaiah and Micah that impinge on our study of divine supremacy and anti-idolatry rhetoric. Isaiah 2:2–4[5] is nearly identical to Mic 4:1–3. The direction of influence between these two well-known texts is difficult to discern. Roberts suggests that the direction of influence is from Isaiah to Micah but ultimately finds the issue irresolvable.[75] In addition, the texts may have a common source.[76] Whether common source or originating with either prophet, it is likely that the texts influenced each other. For our purposes, the possible reuse of Mic 4:5 in Isa 2:5 also deserves attention. Both Isaiah and Micah attached these verses to the preceding units to create a bridge to what follows:[77]

Isaiah 2:5
O house of Jacob, *come*, let us *walk* in YHWH's light.

בֵּית יַעֲקֹב לְכוּ וְנֵלְכָה בְּאוֹר יְהוָה׃

Micah 2:5
For all the nations *walk*, each in the name of its gods. But we will *walk* in the name of YHWH our God forever.

כִּי כָּל־הָעַמִּים יֵלְכוּ אִישׁ בְּשֵׁם אֱלֹהָיו וַאֲנַחְנוּ נֵלֵךְ בְּשֵׁם־יְהוָה אֱלֹהֵינוּ לְעוֹלָם וָעֶד׃

At first glance, the similarities between Isa 2:5 and Mic 2:5b may seem few in number. However, given the roughly identical relationship between Isa 2:2–4 and Mic 2:1–3, the likelihood that these texts either stem from a common source or are genetically related increases. They both contain a double use of the verbal root הלך, an assertion about what "we" (should) do, and a subordinate בְּ clause containing a reference to יהוה. But whereas Mic 2:5b asserts what Judah will do, Isaiah implores Israel to walk in YHWH's light. The most significant difference,

---

74. It may also be noted that Assyria would then fall "but not by a human sword—a sword not made by humans would devour them" (בחרב לא־איש וחרב לא־אדם; v. 8).
75. Roberts, *First Isaiah*, 40.
76. See Gray, "Kingship of God," 15 (cited in Motyer, *Prophecy of Isaiah*, 53).
77. Roberts, *First Isaiah*, 43–44.

however, lies in what Isaiah lacks—Micah's reference to the nations' gods. While we cannot be certain that Isaiah was aware of Micah's reference to the gods, the omission fits with First Isaiah's broader tendency either to omit or to dysphemize the nations' אלהים. For Isaiah, the nations have no אלהים in whose name they might walk.

End of Chapter Reflections

In sum, Isa 2 demonstrates the extent to which (1) anti-image-maker rhetoric took distinctive shape in First Isaiah, and (2) the extent to which anti-image rhetoric is not the exclusive domain of Deutero-Isaiah or the Deuteronomistic literature. In fact, First Isaiah developed its own way of mocking and discrediting the so-called "gods" that appears in only scattered form throughout the rest of the Hebrew Bible. To that end, this study suggests a need to appreciate the distinctive variety of anti-image(-maker) rhetoric in the Hebrew Bible, and in First Isaiah specifically. We cannot do full justice to First Isaiah's rhetoric by simply plotting it on a timeline of development that led inexorably toward Second Isaiah's "full" and "complete" critique of idols and assertion of monotheism. Instead, I suggest in this chapter, and will throughout the rest of this book, that First Isaiah had a full and robust critique of its own, which flowered alongside a remarkable emphasis on YHWH's categorical distinctiveness.

Isaiah 2 occupies a unique and important place in Isaiah's final form. Though some verses may derive from a postexilic context, large portions of vv. 6–22 are most likely original to First Isaiah. The relative dating of these texts is not my concern here, but rather it is the claim that, from a literary perspective, Isa 2:6–22 introduces many of the key themes that then occupy the author in the rest of the book. In other words, Isa 2:6–22 serves an important theological function for the writer, anticipating the exalted vision of YHWH in 6:1–13 and asserting YHWH's supremacy over all self-exalting opponents, including idols.

Moreover, a strong emphasis on YHWH's lofty exaltation accompanies the anti-idol language in Isa 2. The poem in vv. 12–17 that sits at the center of Isa 2 emphasizes YHWH's uncompromising opposition to all who raise themselves up. As a consequence, the idols tremble and are ultimately discarded. The two moves go hand in hand. Because YHWH is exalted on high, there is no place for the idols.

Finally, I suggested that Isa 2 draws together anti-idol themes and ideas that appear scattered across Isa 1–35. Though anti-idolatry rhetoric does not dominate chs. 1–35 like it does chs. 43–46, the emphasis on this theme in Isa 2:6–22 lends the theme greater prominence than it would otherwise have. Moreover, it casts the book's anti-treaty theme in an anti-idol light. Together with the striking divine exaltation language in these verses, the vivid poetry pulls the reader into a scene where they, too, dispose of their idols before the one who arrives to "terrify the earth."

CHAPTER 3

Enemy Boasts and Prophetic Response in Isaiah 10

THE PREVIOUS CHAPTER EXAMINED THE important place that Isa 2:6–22 occupies within First Isaiah. I suggested that the passage foregrounds YHWH's lofty exaltation and the fraudulent nature of so-called deities. This sets the stage for the assertion of YHWH's exalted status throughout First Isaiah and beyond. When considered within the broader context of Isa 1–39, the fourfold use of אלילים in Isa 2 suggests a deliberately derisive rhetorical strategy aimed at undermining trust in false gods in the face of YHWH's uncompromising exaltation, which the book appears eager to underscore. This derisive rhetoric reappears on occasion throughout First Isaiah, though one can hardly call it pervasive. Instead, as suggested earlier, Isa 2:6–22 is an interpretive passage. It interprets Israel's illicit political loyalties and rebellion through the lens of idolatry and then pits those loyalties against YHWH's supremacy, thus emphasizing the importance of YHWH's political supremacy. This will become especially important in Isa 10.

The twofold use of the term אלילים suggests that Isa 10:10–11 belongs to the same thematic strand as Isa 2:6–22.[1] Isaiah 10 thus forms a logical passage for exegetical analysis to test the thesis that First Isaiah exhibits a tendency to assert YHWH's categorical supremacy and simultaneously strip the "gods" of their alleged divine status. As I hope to demonstrate, Isa 10 asserts YHWH's supremacy vis-à-vis Assyrian power using the theme of idolatry, but with a new twist. In Isa 10, the boasting Assyrian king claims that he would do to Jerusalem and its אלילים as he had done to Samaria and the nations (vv. 8–11). Assyria simultaneously asserts Yahwistic teaching and overreaches by assuming Jerusalem's deity was one of the "images." YHWH's quid-pro-quo response reduces Assyria to a (mere) club (v. 5) or ax (v. 15) in his hands, a thing made of wood. To that extent, Isaiah shows the ways that Assyria is a false object of ultimate trust.

This chapter proceeds along the following lines. First, I suggest that vv. 10–12 provide an interpretive key for vv. 5–19, which reframes Assyria's affront to YHWH in terms of blasphemy. Assyria equates YHWH with the non-deities of the nations. YHWH then turns the tables to suggest that Assyria is, like idols, an object of wood that its political superior wields. Second, I suggest that those same verses, in conjunction with vv. 8–9, reuse material from Isa 36–37 but

---

1. For an argument for a close literary and structural relationship between chs. 2 and 10, see Blum, "Jesajas prophetisches Testament"; Williamson, "Idols in Isaiah."

intentionally remove references to the אלהים, thus highlighting Isaiah's aversion to the word אלהים. Finally, I examine the continuation of the theme of YHWH's political supremacy with an analysis of the unique divine name האדון in Isa 10:16 and 33.

Redaction in 10:5–19

Isaiah 10 is a pivotal chapter in First Isaiah. It offers the most sustained series of judgment oracles against a *foreign* nation in the book thus far. Prior to ch. 10, the prophet directed most of his oracular invectives against Judah/Jerusalem, with occasional prophesies against the Northern Kingdom (e.g., 7:8; 9:8–21), and only the briefest of threats against other nations (e.g., 5:30). Assyria heretofore played a decidedly negative role in carrying out God's plans to judge Judah (7:20; 8:7). Isaiah 10:5–19 portrays the Assyrian king as the "rod" of YHWH's wrath and as an imperious tyrant who exceeds his mandate. The Assyrian king had indeed been commissioned by YHWH, but then he hatched his own plans (v. 7). He planned to destroy nations with reckless abandon and claimed that his own strength carried him thus far (v. 13–14). The claim to autonomous power gave rise to a prophetic response in the form of initial questions (v. 15) and a prophetic judgment oracle (vv. 16–19).

As is often the case in Isaiah, 10:5–19 displays a rich web of allusions with other passages in the book. Those allusions are not simply cross-referencing other similar sounding texts. They also *modify* perspectives on similar themes found elsewhere. For instance, whereas thus far in the book Assyria was an agent of divine judgment, Isa 10 offers a fresh word that Assyria would become a recipient of divine judgment. Such shifting policies toward Assyria suggest to some that First Isaiah reflects the kind of "real time" prophetic dispatches that one might expect in the middle of the Assyrian crises of the early eighth century, even if they were redacted at a later point.[2] Hermann Barth and others, for instance, assign the bulk of these verses to a Neo-Assyrian inner core that was later appended and redacted in the later Babylonian period (e.g., Isa 13:1–14a, 22–23; and 21:1–10).[3]

With the exception of vv. 10–11, the passage focuses on Assyrian arrogance and military ambition. But vv. 10–11 introduce a new theme, relating to idolatry:

---

2. Sweeney, *Isaiah 1–39*, 206; Roberts, *First Isaiah*, 165–166; Aster, *Reflections of Empire*, 173–83.

3. See Carr, *Formation of the Hebrew Bible*, 327, who writes, "In sum, embedded in Isaiah 1–11 (aside from the above surveyed late materials) is a set of texts (1:21–26; 2:12–19*; 3:1–17, 24; 5:1–29; [6–8*]; 9:7–10:4 [ET 9:8–10:4]; 10:5–15; 10:33–11:9), each of which has some claim to be Isaianic, which in turn are part of a broader concentric structure which likely also is Isaianic."

Just as my hand found the kingdoms of the fraud god,[4] whose images were more numerous than Jerusalem and Samaria. . . . Indeed, I shall do to Jerusalem and its idols just as I have done to Samaria and its fraud gods. (Isa 10:10–11)[5]

The precise nature of his claim is debated among interpreters. It is not clear if the Assyrian king equates YHWH with idols or if he is seen as an iconoclast who plans to wipe out the idols of Samaria and Jerusalem. I will deal with this question below, when considering the relationship between vv. 8–12 and Isa 36–37. For now, however, it is simply important to register the question and consider the redactional status of vv. 10–11.

The shift in emphasis in vv. 10–11 suggests to many scholars that these verses are editorial insertions. There are several reasons for this, which Williamson outlines in some detail.[6] I offer here several pieces in his argument, which I then evaluate. First, the sequence in vv. 5–9 "reaches its climax with Samaria."[7] The shift to Jerusalem (v. 10) and Zion (v. 11) seem out of place. Second, the shift in the basis for judgment from vv. 5–9 and 10–11 is significant enough to suspect secondary insertion. Verses 5–9 focus on arrogance, and then vv. 10–11 on idolatry. Third, v. 13 continues the Assyrian boast quite naturally from v. 9.[8] To this we can add Siegfried Mittmann's observation that vv. 5–9 and 13–14 exhibit a very similar 3 + 3 poetic structure.[9] Williamson also notes the unusual syntax of vv. 10–11. Fourth, Williamson argues that the phrases מצאה ידי ל- ("my hand has found/struck out against") and use of עשיתי and אעשה ("I have acted/I will act") in v. 11 seem dependent on similar language in vv. 13–14 and may thus be secondary.

While Williamson's first, second, and fourth points are weak on their own, in conjunction with his third point, his argument gains strength. His first two claims depend on topical and thematic shifts, which are frequent in poetry. While it is possible that vv. 10–11 depend on vv. 13–14 (see my fourth point in the previous paragraph) and are therefore later, as the semantic similarities are striking, it is reasonable that a poet would plan a theme and then signal that theme at an earlier point in the poem. Unfortunately, Williamson and others (Becker makes the same observation) do not discuss evidence for direction of influence between vv. 10–11 and vv. 13–14. They only assert it. I am therefore hesitant to accept Williamson's fourth point as evidence for the secondary

---

4. Most translations render this as a plural, so, "idols" (e.g., JPS, NRSV, NIV, ESV), even though the MT has a singular האליל. 1QIsaᵃ has האלילים, apparently trying to bring clarity and alignment with plural ופסליהם in the same verse.
5. Ellipses original.
6. Williamson, "Idols in Isaiah," 17–28.
7. Ibid., 17.
8. Ibid., 20.
9. Mittmann, "'Wehe! Assur, Stab meines Zorn,'" 112–13.

status of vv. 10–11. However, the tight 3 + 3 or 3 + 4 poetry in vv. 5–9 and 13–15 does raise questions about possible insertions in vv. 10–11. When set alongside the observation that v. 12 is prose, and very likely secondary, editorial activity becomes even more plausible. In fact, Wildberger observes that vv. 10–11 are likely prose, "in spite of the metrical arrangement found in BHK and BHS."[10]

A final plank in Williamson's argument, and one most relevant for our study, is his suggestion that the concern over idols (אלילים and עצבים) in vv. 10–11 are secondary and in fact occasion the insertion of these verses into the passage. Williamson is in good company here, as Childs, Barth, Vermeylen, Blum, Becker, Wildberger and others have argued similarly.[11] As noted in ch. 1, Williamson assigns these idolatry additions in vv. 10–11 to a unified redactional layer in First Isaiah.[12] My purpose is not to recover the date of such insertions, if that is the best way to understand them. They may originate from a time earlier than scholars often assume.[13] Nevertheless, the possible addition of the verses raises the possibility that Isaiah is not only editing its immediate context but also anticipating or responding to ideas expressed elsewhere in the work.

One such possibility emerges when we consider Isa 10:10–11 in relation to Isa 36–37, which freely employs the term אלהים. If it can be shown that vv. 10–11 depend on Isa 36–37 but substitute אלילים for אלהים, then we have further evidence that First Isaiah, or an editor thereof, exhibits the kind of deity aversion I have suggested.

The Relationship Between Isaiah 10:8–11 and 36–37

The following charts outline several key similarities between Isa 10:8–11 and Isa 36 (with parallels in 2 Kgs 18), with corresponding elements in bold type, underlined, and italic type.

Isaiah 10
Is not Calno like Carchemesh? Is not <u>Hamath</u> like Arphad? Is not <u>Samaria</u> like Damascus?

Isaiah 36–37
Where are the **gods** of <u>Hamath</u> and Arpad? Where are the **gods** of Sepharvaim? Have they delivered

---

10. Wildberger, *Isaiah 1–12*, 414.
11. Childs, *Isaiah and the Assyrian Crisis*, 42–43, followed by Barth, *Die Jesaja-Worte*, 23; Vermeylen, *Du Prophète Isaïe*, 255; Blum, "Jesajas prophetisches Testament," 560; Becker, *Jesaja*, 202; Bäckersten, *Isaiah's Political Message*, 153–54, noted by Williamson, "Idols in Isaiah," 20; Wildberger, *Isaiah 1–12*, 413–14.
12. Cf. Kaiser, *Isaiah 1–12*, 232, who argues that idols do not account for the insertion of vv. 10–12.
13. Note the possible interaction with Assyrian ideology, outlined by Aster, *Reflections of Empire*.

Just as **my hand** found the *kingdoms* of the **fraud god(s)**, whose **images** were more numerous than Jerusalem and Samaria. . . . Indeed, I shall do to Jerusalem and its **fraud gods** just as I have done to Samaria and its **idols**.	Samaria out of **my hand**? Who among all the **gods** of these countries have saved their countries out of **my hand**, that the LORD should save Jerusalem out of **my hand**?
כַּאֲשֶׁר מָצְאָה יָדִי לְמַמְלְכֹת הָאֱלִיל וּפְסִילֵיהֶם מִירוּשָׁלִַם וּמִשֹּׁמְרוֹן: הֲלֹא כַּאֲשֶׁר עָשִׂיתִי לְשֹׁמְרוֹן וְלֶאֱלִילֶיהָ כֵּן אֶעֱשֶׂה לִירוּשָׁלִַם וְלַעֲצַבֶּיהָ: (Isa 10:10–11)	אַיֵּה אֱלֹהֵי חֲמָת וְאַרְפָּד אַיֵּה אֱלֹהֵי סְפַרְוָיִם וְכִי־הִצִּילוּ אֶת־שֹׁמְרוֹן מִיָּדִי: מִי בְּכָל־אֱלֹהֵי הָאֲרָצוֹת הָאֵלֶּה אֲשֶׁר־הִצִּילוּ אֶת־אַרְצָם מִיָּדִי כִּי־יַצִּיל יְהוָה אֶת־יְרוּשָׁלִַם מִיָּדִי: (Isa 36:19–20)
Has any of the **gods** of the nations ever delivered its land out of the hand of the king of Assyria? Where are the **gods** of Hamath and Arpad? Where are the **gods** of Sepharvaim, Hena, and Ivvah? Have they delivered Samaria out of **my hand**? (2 Kgs 18:33–34)	Have the **gods** of the nations delivered them, the nations that my predecessors destroyed, Gozan, Haran, Rezeph, and the people of Eden who were in Telassar? Where is the *king* of Hamath, the *king* of Arpad, the *king* of the city of Sepharvaim, the *king* of Hena, or the *king* of Ivvah? (Isa 37:12–13)

Several details from this comparison deserve mention. First, there is a clear relationship between Isa 10:9–11 and Isa 36:19. The degree to which the editor of First Isaiah was aware of 2 Kgs 18:33 remains uncertain, though similar connections exist there as well. The points of connection include location (Hamath and Arpad), reference to "my hand," as well as the (non-)deities of various locales. Second, the relationship is not explainable simply in terms of one large quotation. Rather, Isa 10 appears to draw from a whole range of lexica and themes present 36:19–20 especially, but also in 37:12–13 and possibly 2 Kgs 18:33. Third, and most significant for our purposes, Isa 10:9–11 avoids any reference to אלהים, despite their presence in 36:19–20 (3×), 37:12–13 (1×), and 2 Kings 18:33 (3×). If Isa 10:11 is indeed redactional (or 10:10–11), and interacting with Isa 36–37, the possibility of substitution becomes strong. In addition to substituting אלילים for אלהים, the writer of Isa 10 also includes the terms פסלים (images) and עצבים (idols). This rich lexical concentration on non-deities when drawing from texts that make reference to other deities is striking.

Blenkinsopp and others have observed that the parallels between Isa 10:10–11 and Isa 36–37 are not alone. A range of parallels between other portions of Isa 10 and 36–37 also exist as part of a larger and "deliberate structuring device" that brings chs. 7–12 and 36–39 into parallel.[14] This structuring device is well known in Isaian scholarship, though the scope and extent of it is debated.[15] The present text, however, likely foreshadows the events and attitudes of the Assyrian king in chs. 36–39 but reframes it in terms of blasphemy against YHWH. The Assyrian misjudges Jerusalem on the basis of the nations and their weak idols and assumes that Jerusalem would be only as strong as the number of its idols. Judging from the ease with which he trampled the nations, and the fact that they had more idols than Samaria and Jerusalem, Jerusalem would easily fall (vv. 10–11).

Few commentators have noted the clear aversion to language of divinity in Isa 10, and even fewer have explained whether these verses reflect dependency or shared material. Though a consensus now exists that Isa 10:8–11 are modeled on the Rabshakeh's language in Isa 36–37 (cf. 2 Kgs 18–19), earlier scholarship had long assumed the opposite, that Isa 10 influenced chs. 36–39.[16] The reasons for this were apparently obvious. Isaiah 10 comes earlier in the book, and vv. 9–11 sit amidst material that looks quite early. Scholarly opinion has now shifted, such that now "a reverse direction of influence is also possible."[17] Childs suggests that vv. 8–11 likely depend on chs. 36–37 and thus postdate the 701 crisis.[18] He observes how vv. 10–11 add the offense of blasphemy to the Assyrian king's offenses. Not only had the king exceeded his directives, but he had "included [YHWH] with the impotent pagan gods."[19]

Watts suggests that vv. 8–11 depend on the Rabshakeh's speeches found in 2 Kgs 18–19 and in Isa 36–37 but does not specify which specific verses. He notes that while they depend on these passages, they function differently. Rather than "psychological warfare," they "illustrate the Assyrian's attitude and character."[20]

For Becker, Isa 10 depends on Isa 36–39 and is not simply drawing from a common tradition. Like Childs, he cites a number of commentators for whom the direction of influence goes in the other direction.[21] However, Becker finds it more likely that the direction of influence is toward de-deifying. To explain the *addition* of Carchemish, Calno, and Damascus in Isa 10, he suggests that "Carchemish and Calno have possibly been inserted because here the alliteration is especially marked" (cf. Jer 46:2; Amos 6:2).[22] The author simply inserted a few

14. Blenkinsopp, *Isaiah 1–39*, 253.
15. Childs, *Isaiah*, 266.
16. Ibid., 92.
17. Ibid.
18. Ibid., while the material in vv. 5–9 and 13–19 *predate* the crisis; Becker, *Jesaja*, 209.
19. Childs, *Isaiah*, 92.
20. Watts, *Isaiah 1–33*, 148.
21. Becker, *Jesaja*, 209. Childs, *Isaiah*, 92, notes the same but does not give any references.
22. Becker, *Jesaja*, 209.

cities known from the Assyrian conquest.²³ Becker never explains the omission of certain cities from 37:10–13 in 10:9 and 11, an issue that may raise doubts if one is going to argue persuasively that the verses in Isa 10 are later. Nevertheless, Becker makes an even more convincing case that Isa 10:9, 11* draw from 36:18–20 and 37:10–13, two different stages in the growth of chs. 36–39.²⁴ This renders unlikely the idea that Isa 36–39 draws from Isa 10.

In short, there are reasons to suggest that Isa 10 at least draws from the range of biblical (or extrabiblical) Assyrian rhetoric about Samaria and Jerusalem and likely draws from phrases used in Isa 36–37 but de-deifies the rhetoric. This de-deification reinforces the claim that Assyria swelled with pride (and ignorance), to its own demise. Assyria wrongly assumed that its victories over the nations and Samaria were attributable to its own superior power, and that Jerusalem would be an easy victory because its idols were so few. Assyria failed to recognize its status as a tool in YHWH's hand.

A close relationship between Isa 10:9–11 and Isa 36:18–20 is hard to deny. Both texts refer to the boastful claims of the Assyrian king, the inability of Hamath, Arpad, and Samaria to escape the king's "hand," and end with a rhetorical question about Jerusalem's inability to escape his hand. Because of these similarities, the differences between these verses are striking. Whereas Isa 36 focuses on the inability of the nations' *deities* (אלהי הגוים) and then YHWH to deliver from Sennacherib's hands, Isa 10 focuses on *images*—the אלילים and the עצבים (10:11).

YHWH, the Sovereign (10:16, 33)

After indicting the Assyrian king for his pride and blasphemy, the prophet then turns to announce YHWH's judgment. The Assyrian king had miscalculated. The gods are indeed non-gods, but YHWH is sovereign—or more accurately, *the* sovereign (האדון). Isaiah uses the unique title האדון יהוה צבאות ("the sovereign, YHWH of armies") twice in ch. 10. In the first (v. 16), the prophet announces fiery judgment on his foes. In the second, we hear that YHWH will chop down the loftiest trees "and the exalted will be laid low" (v. 33). With one exception, the title האדון is unique to First Isaiah. It occurs six times in the Hebrew Bible—five of which are in First Isaiah.²⁵ Moreover, the divine name אדני occurs with some frequency in the book and also deserves our attention.²⁶

Johan Lust argues that the title האדון is significant, and that while bearing similarities in use to אדני, it carries a different sense. Lust develops his argument

---

23. Ibid., 209–10.
24. Ibid.
25. Isa 1:24; 3:1; 10:16, 33; 19:4; cf. Mal 3:1 and the form האדן in Exod 23:17; 34:23.
26. Lust, "Divine Titles."

by contrasting Isaiah's use of the title אדני (and האדון) with Ezekiel's. While the name *Adōnai* occurs far more frequently in Ezekiel (217× vs. 25× in Isaiah), only two of Ezekiel's uses occur outside of formulaic contexts.[27] Correspondingly, in Isa 1–39 the term occurs outside formulaic contexts on 15 occasions. Lust suggests that, like in Ezekiel, אדני typically implies the prophet's (or king's) special relationship to YHWH as "my lord," hence the pronominal suffix. By contrast, the otherwise unique האדון "expresses the majesty and universal might of the Lord."[28] In contrast to modern translations, which do not typically distinguish between אדני and האדון, the Septuagint distinguishes them sharply in at least three occasions. It renders האדון as ὁ δεσπότης κύριος (rendering האדון as ὁ δεσπότης and יהוה as κύριος). Moreover, Lust notes that "nowhere in LXX-Isaiah is δεσπότης used as an equivalent of אדני or any form of אדון without the article."[29] Regarding Isa 10, Lust suggests that the "האדון phrases are found in the original sections dealing with the arrogance of Assur" and "again expresses the Lord's majesty and power as a ruler of the world."[30] Lust, following Sweeney's redactional assessment of the chapter, argues that the two titles derive from different redactional layers, with האדון expressing an earlier political confrontation with Assyrian imperial claims.[31] Whether or not one accepts this redactional assessment, his point concerning the *meaning* of האדון is convincing and fits my own assessment of its use in ch. 10 and throughout the book. Specifically, האדון is a designation highlighting YHWH's distinguished political sovereignty.

In addition to Lust's argument concerning the nonformulaic use of the term, we can also observe the unique reference to *other* "lords" in Isa 26:13:

YHWH our God, Lords besides you (אדנים זולתך) have ruled over us,
but we invoke your name alone.

This text forms part of a national confession that spans from 26:12–18. Here, the people acknowledge that though other "Lords" (that is, imperial powers) ruled the people, they acknowledge YHWH alone. Isaiah's reference to "Lords besides you" (אדנים זולתך) bears striking resemblance to the phrase "gods besides you" used elsewhere in the Hebrew Bible.[32] Deutero-Isaiah insists that YHWH was the only one who could deliver: "Except me there is no god" (זולתי אין אלהים; 45:5, 21), and Trito-Isaiah insists that Israel had not seen a "god except you" (אלהים זולתך) since ancient days. The equivalent phrases אלוה מבלעדי ("Is there a

---

27. Ibid., 131.
28. Ibid., 136.
29. Ibid., 133.
30. Ibid., 138, 148.
31. Ibid., 139–41.
32. 2 Sam 7:22 // 1 Chr 17:20; Isa 45:5, 21; 64:3; Hos 13:4 (cf. Isa 43:11; 44:8; 2 Sam 22:32).

god besides me?" Isa 44:8) and אין (אלהים) עוד מלבדו ("There is no god besides him"; Deut 4:35) appear elsewhere. The occurrence of אדנים instead of אלהים in Isa 26:13 is thus something of an outlier compared to these texts in Second Isaiah and Deuteronomy. The differences highlight the political qualities of First Isaiah's *monotheizing*. This form of monotheizing sets YHWH's supremacy in relation to other rulers, and not just other alleged deities. YHWH is האדון, "the sovereign," despite Israel's political submission to other אדנים.

Evidence from elsewhere in the Hebrew Bible also points to the idea the non-suffixed אדון refers to political sovereignty and power. In contrast to אדני, technically "my lord," אדון occurs infrequently. It occurs only eleven times in the Hebrew Bible, and only six refer to YHWH. The other five uses are purely secular. Significantly, the anarthrous form אדון consistently highlights YHWH's *cosmic lordship*. Joshua 3:11 and 13 use the unique form אדון to emphasize YHWH's supreme Lordship. In those texts, the Joshua instructs the people to ready themselves since "the ark of the covenant of YHWH, Lord of all the earth" (ארון הברית אדון כל־הארץ) would pass before them. Using the same construction, Ps 97:5 describes mountains melting "before YHWH ... Lord of all the earth" (אדון כל־הארץ; cf. Ps 114:7). Zechariah describes visions in which he sees two olive trees beside the lampstand, which represent two anointed figures before "the Lord of all the earth" (אדון כל־הארץ; Zech 4:14). Later, the angel describes four spirits who had stood before "the Lord of all the earth" (אדון כל־הארץ; 6:5). Five of these six examples use the phrase אדון כל־הארץ, and each of those five refers to YHWH's cultic presence, which fit with Isaiah's emphasis on YHWH's presence in Zion.

Several additional comments about the significance of האדון are in order. First, the basic meaning of האדון is relatively clear. It means "the Lord," or "the sovereign," and seems to carry specific connotations relating to divine rule and authority in Zion.[33] First Isaiah's rendering of the more commonly formulated epithet אדני + sphere of rule (i.e., "Lord of...") into a stand-alone epithet with the definite article and a divine title in apposition is paralleled by his use of the term המלך in 6:5. There, the prophet sees YHWH enthroned in the temple and calls him המלך יהוה צבאות ("the king, YHWH of armies"). The parallel runs deeper. Isaiah deploys the title האדון *only* in association with the phrase יהוה צבאות, suggesting that the title האדון may carry military overtones. This would make sense in an environment where YHWH's sovereignty was questioned and challenged by the Assyrian king, who refers to himself as "the great king" (Isa 36:4, 12) enthroned in Zion. With the exception of 1:24 and 3:1, the three other occurrences of האדון appear in connection with YHWH's military action against or through Assyria (10:16, 33; 19:4). The occurrence of such claims in relation to

---

33. Wildberger, *Isaiah 1–12*, 69.

Assyria are not surprising. Assyrian kings regularly assumed the status of "great king" along with a slew of related claims. For instance, in a building inscription from Calah, Ashurnasirpal II (884–859) calls himself "The Great King, the mighty king, the king of the universe."[34] Sargon II (722–705) later adopts the very same title and also includes the common epithet "king of the four quarters/regions (of the world)."[35] The titling only continues with Sennacherib, Isaiah's contemporary. This from his annals (the Taylor Prism):

> Sennacherib, the great king, the mighty king, king of the universe, king of Assyria, king of the four quarters (of the earth); the wise ruler . . . favorite of the great gods, guardian of the right, lover of justice; who lends support, who comes to the aid of the needy, who turns (his thoughts) to pious deeds; perfect hero, mighty man; first among all princes, the flame that consumes the insubmissive, who strikes the wicked with the thunderbolt.[36]

As Peter Machinist, Shawn Aster, Michael Chan, and others have argued, First Isaiah frequently imitates Assyrian royal campaign rhetoric to describe YHWH's actions against his enemies.[37] It is possible that the sole "Lordship" of YHWH emphasized through this term is yet another inflection of Assyrian claims to supremacy. It is the nations, after all, whose claims to supremacy YHWH consistently counters in First Isaiah.

For instance, YHWH's campaigns into the forested mountains reflect knowledge of Assyrian imperial rhetoric. Tiglath-pileser's annals give one example of many forest cutting reports: "I went to Mount Lebanon, trunks of cedar. . . . I cut, I carried off."[38] Shalmaneser III, from his throne base at Calah he reports: "I ascended the Amanus range (and) cut down beams of cedar (and) juniper."[39] The kings would take the heroic journey to the west in order to acquire trees for their temples. However, the journeys were more ideologically than practically driven. These westward journeys were considered acts of bravery, and as Aster explains, they became a way to prove "kingliness."[40] But in Isa 10:33–34, rather than the Assyrian King, it is YHWH who takes the heroic westward journey to

---

34. Luckenbill, *Ancient Records*, 1:193–94.
35. Ibid., 2:25, 47, 56, 60, and elsewhere.
36. Ibid., 2:115.
37. Machinist, "Assyria," 719–37; Aster, "Image of Assyria," 249–78; Aster, "Transmission of Neo-Assyrian Claims"; Aster, *Reflections*, 225–34; Chan, "Rhetorical Reversal and Usurpation"; Malamat, "Campaigns to the Mediterranean"; Sweeney, "Sargon's Threat"; Cohen, "Neo-Assyrian Elements."
38. RIMA 2:37; Aster, *Reflections*, 232.
39. Chan, "Rhetorical Reversal," 731.
40. Aster, *Reflections*, 231.

chop down trees. According to Michael Chan: "The reversal in 10:33–34, then, is quite simple: instead of the Assyrian king taking the glorious and ideologically freighted westward journey, it will be YHWH, the heroic earth-scorching siege warrior (10:16–19), who will cut down the age-old cedars of Lebanon."[41] YHWH has appropriated the show of kingliness for himself. He is "the Sovereign."

These comparative studies sharpen our understanding of the exclusive nature of YHWH's sovereignty. The title האדון appears to be a relatively unique term by which some Proto-Isaian texts assert YHWH's sovereignty in relation to other humans, typically kings, who raise themselves above YHWH. Just as some other biblical texts append ה- before אלהים to emphasize YHWH's sole divinity,[42] אדון + ה- signals YHWH's *sole political sovereignty*. To that end, the prophet employs the title האדון in concert with imagery that reflects familiarity with Assyrian political rhetoric. These are some of the most forceful and violent images of divine power in First Isaiah: "Look, The Sovereign (האדון), YHWH of armies is lopping off the crowns of the trees with shocking force. The highest of the heights he is cutting down, and the lofty will be laid low" (10:33). This verse returns us to the type of exaltation and abasement rhetoric we observed in full force in Isa 2 and in 5:15–16.[43] As sole political sovereign, for whom supremacy is displayed in terms of *height*, he brooks no rival. The scene recalls the tree-chopping campaigns of YHWH evident in 2:12–13, 9:17, and 10:16–19. YHWH once again takes to the mountains in order to cut down trees and all the height(s) (הקומה), and to bring low the proud.

Rhetorically, the effect of YHWH's tree-chopping campaign (Isa 10:33–34) is powerful. Notice how Isa 10:28–32 portrays the preparations, advancement, and terror of an unnamed military commander. Commentators regularly strain to identify the specific Assyrian campaign in view.[44] But the passage is unyielding, and perhaps for good reason. YHWH's opposition is not just to a particular Assyrian king or a certain Assyrian campaign. Instead, he opposes *all* that exalts itself. YHWH's tree-chopping connects the passage back to other occasions where God brings down the powerful "trees of the forest" (2:12–13; 9:17; 10:15; 37:24), in whatever form they might take. Childs captures the significance of YHWH's abasement of this unnamed enemy: "The portrait of this colossus moving swiftly and with consummate ease over every possible barrier, and then emerging on the very outskirts of the city to shake its fist at Mount Zion,

---

41. Chan, "Isaiah 10:5–34," 732.
42. See also Rendtorff, "'*El* als israelitische Gottesbezeichnung," esp. pp. 14–21. First Isaiah's penchant for adding arthrous titles to the militarized יהוה צבאות appears also in 5:16 with the title האל הקדוש, "the holy God," or, "the God, the Holy One," which occurs in parallel to the title יהוה צבאות.
43. Cf. 2:13–14, and see appendix 2, pp. 108–9.
44. See Sweeney, "Sargon's Threat"; Childs, *Isaiah*, 96.

borders on the mythological."[45] While the passage hints at specific historical circumstances (named cities, etc.), YHWH's totalizing attack on this unnamed "tall tree" suggests that the prophet is using this circumstance to epitomize YHWH's general sovereignty and power over the mighty nations of the earth, whoever they might be, who oppose his work in Zion.

Fourth, Wildberger argues that the title יהוה צבאות was rooted, with the title האדון צבאות, in the cultic traditions originating in Shiloh, which conceptualized YHWH enthroned above the ark in his sanctuary.[46] According to Wildberger, Isaiah wanted to emphasize that "the God of Jerusalem is the same God as the one who once was worshiped in Shiloh at the former center of the amphictyony."[47] While the desire for continuity may have been a concern of Isaiah's, this type of argument runs the risk of equating original meaning with the meaning in Isaiah's day, a type of genetic fallacy. It must be noted that, unlike Jeremiah, Isaiah shows no interest in the link to Shiloh.[48] And while the צבאות tradition may have originated at Shiloh (cf. 1 Sam 1:3, 11), Isaiah and his audience were not necessarily aware of that tradition-historical connection. Yet, despite difficulty ascertaining Isaiah's awareness of this putative early tradition, it is noteworthy that יהוה צבאות occurs frequently in conjunction with proclamations of YHWH's *kingship*, both in those early texts and in Isaiah itself.[49]

Horst Preuss also points out that the appellative יהוה צבאות, which he renders "YHWH of hosts," or in the abstract, "YHWH of powerfulness," occurs frequently in connection with the Zion tradition. Indeed, the title יהוה צבאות occurs together with ציון eleven times in Isa 1–39, far more than any other book except Zechariah.[50] Moreover, it is frequently "combined with the predication of YHWH as king."[51] The most notable and striking example in First Isaiah comes from Isa 37:16, in which the prophet refers to "YHWH of armies [יהוה צבאות], God of Israel" who is "enthroned above the cherubim." The prophet goes on to praise him: "You indeed alone are God" (Isa 37:16).[52] This hints that Isaianic claims about YHWH's supremacy relate to his cultic enthronement and appearance as king.

---

45. Childs, *Isaiah*, 97.
46. Wildberger, *Isaiah 1–12*, 68; cf. Mettinger, *Dethronement of Sabaoth*.
47. Wildberger, *Isaiah 1–12*, 68.
48. Jer 7:12, 14; 26:6, 9; 41:5.
49. See references and discussion in Preuss, *Old Testament Theology*, 1:146.
50. Adjusted proportionately. Isaiah has a higher number of cases (11 hits), though the density is higher in Zechariah. Isa 1:8; 3:16, 17; 8:18; 10:24, 32; 18:7; 24:23; 29:8; 31:4; 37:32. Cf. Zech 1:14, 17; 2:7, 10; 8:2, 3; 9:13. I ran this search on occurrences of ציון within one verse of יהוה צבאות.
51. Preuss, *Old Testament Theology*, 146. Preuss cites as examples Ps 24:10; 46:8, 12; 48:9; 84:2, 4, 9, 13; 89:9; Isa 6:3, 5; 8:18; and 31:4.
52. אתה־הוא האלהים לבדך.

Finally, First Isaiah appears to foreground and cluster unique divine names in the early part of the book. The title האדון occurs first in 1:24, within a string of divine appellatives—האדון יהוה צבאות אביר ישראל. Like the judgment oracle in 10:16, where האדון also occurs, the verse begins with the result particle לכן. This particle suggests that this verse plays a culminating role in the first chapter of Isaiah. In Isa 1:24, the sovereignty title occurs next to another unique title אביר ישראל (otherwise אביר יעקב).[53] The phrase אביר ישראל refers in several contexts to the power of mighty bulls or stallions that threaten and trample.[54] Appropriately, 1:24 is the first display of divine force against enemies in the book (cf. v. 20) and thus serves as an appropriate place to assert YHWH's supremacy over the nations through these unique titles. In other words, two unique Isaian appellatives occur together at the beginning of the book, and both emphasize YHWH's strength and rule. Placed beside the otherwise unique אביר ישראל, it seems clear that Isaiah is self-consciously drawing attention to a distinctive name—one that emphasizes YHWH's strength and rule. As the first display of divine force and threat against enemies in the book (cf. v. 20), it thus serves as an appropriate "lead off" description of YHWH's supremacy over the nations.

The Sovereign King

The assertion of YHWH's exclusive sovereignty ties Isa 10 and its congeners to the broader theme of divine kingship in the book of Isaiah. Isaiah 6:5 refers to "*the* king YHWH (המלך יהוה צבאות) of hosts," who is sitting "high and lofty" on his throne. Berges observes how YHWH's lofty enthronement is a "counterimage" to the Judean kings in chs. 1–5. This divine title "is more significant than it appears at first glance," Berges notes, since 2:12–14 uses the phrase "high and lofty" to contrast all that YHWH abases.[55] In the light of Isa 2, Isa 6:5 takes on significance beyond Judah: "The lofty monarchy of God . . . is a critique rather than a legitimation of human claims to power." Whether we are to understand this in totalizing terms is uncertain. However, the Assyrian king is a "counterimage," to use Berges's term.[56]

This concept applies also to the Babylonian king in Isa 14, where rhetoric of abasement and exaltation abounds. In Isa 14:11–19 alone the roots *עלה (ascend) and *ירד (descend) occur three times each, the highest concentration of either

---

53. Isa 49:26; 60:16.
54. Isa 34:7; Ps 22:13; 68:31; Judg 5:22. See discussion in Roberts, *First Isaiah*, 28–29. Roberts translates the phrase אביר ישראל "Mighty Bull of Israel."
55. Berges, "Kingship and Servanthood," 163; cf. Schultz, "King in the Book of Isaiah."
56. Berges, "Kingship and Servanthood," 169.

in the book.⁵⁷ They describe the king's ascent to the "heights" where he raised his throne to the stars of God. Yet he falls from heaven and is cast to the earth. As Berges notes, the king of Babylon is a "cipher for all oppressive rulers." His demise brings rest and prosperity to the whole world (14:6–8), while the great rulers descend to the underworld and meet "all who were kings of the nations" (14:9) and are exposed in all their weakness (14:10, 12–19). The critique of other royal claims continues throughout First Isaiah. For instance, at the end of the oracles against the nations, "all the kingdoms of the earth" receive their due. Then, in Isa 24–27, YHWH punishes the hosts of heaven and "the kings of the earth" (24:21).⁵⁸ Finally, First Isaiah culminates with YHWH's defeat of Sennacherib on Zion (Isa 36–39). Berges summarizes First Isaiah's perspective: "YHWH is *the* king of the world (Isa 6). He reveals himself over and against *all the kingdoms of the earth* as a powerful savior and the one and only God."⁵⁹ Isaiah's rhetoric of abasement serves as a powerful reminder of YHWH's exclusive political supremacy.

Isaiah's opposition to all oppressive rulers accompanies a reticence even toward the promised ideal ruler of Israel, who is never called "king" (Isa 7, 9, 11).⁶⁰ While Isaiah clearly contains messianic hopes, it does so in a way that maintains due deference to YHWH's exclusive royal prerogatives and exclusive sovereignty. These exclusivist royal claims prepare the way for Deutero-Isaiah, where the term *king* is only used of YHWH in the singular (41:21; 43:15; 44:6; 52:7). The "kings" of the nations are duly humbled and abased.⁶¹ While Isaiah does not erase entirely the legitimacy of a righteous Judean ruler, he certainly asserts divine kingship with such fervor that the claims of all rival אדנים end in the dust.

Conclusions

In conclusion, I have argued in this chapter that the use of הָאָדוֹן in First Isaiah reflects the book's wider emphasis on YHWH's sole sovereignty vis-à-vis the nations. Whereas Deutero-Isaiah emphasizes YHWH's distinctiveness primarily in relation to idol makers and other deities,⁶² Proto-Isaiah asserts YHWH's political power and exclusive claim on Israel and the nations. We have seen that Isa 10

---

57. This is discussed in appendix 2.
58. Berges, "Kingship," 169.
59. Ibid.
60. With the possible exception of 32:1 ("A king will reign in righteousness"), which 33:17 and 22 clarify as a reference to YHWH, not a human ruler (ibid., 168).
61. Ibid., 169–70.
62. MacDonald, "Monotheism and Isaiah."

continues deploying spatial rhetoric of exaltation and abasement. YHWH intends to abase the human powers that raise themselves up to an exalted place. First Isaiah underscores YHWH's sole sovereignty in conjunction with the abasement of the self-aggrandizing Assyrians. The reference to אלילים in vv. 10–11 reflects Assyria's ignorance about YHWH's categorical distinctiveness. The Assyrian king is used by God to declaim the fraudulent quality of the nations' gods, but he goes too far, forgetting that YHWH is not just one of the nations' gods. In fact, he is "the Sovereign, YHWH of armies" who lays rightful claim to the Assyrian—and indeed all imperial—declarations of power over the mighty trees of the high mountain forests and heights.

CHAPTER 4

The Folly of the Gods in Isaiah 19

UNDERSTANDING THE MEANING AND SIGNIFICANCE of the אלילים draws us into the sapiential world of First Isaiah, a world about which we have not yet spoken in this book. Scholars have long noted the prominence of wisdom in First Isaiah and debated its significance for interpreting chs. 1–35.[1] Wisdom themes emerge in description of YHWH's wise but mysterious plan with Assyria, but even more strongly in passages that critique the so-called "wise."[2] Just as First Isaiah employs a rhetoric of abasement to juxtapose YHWH's exaltation, he critiques the "wise" to foreground YHWH's superior wisdom. Accordingly, First Isaiah emphasizes YHWH's willingness to sabotage human faculties of perception as an act of judgment.[3] This chapter considers the use of אלילים within the context of Isaiah's critique of human folly and judgment on human faculties of perception. I focus on the use of אלילים in Isa 19:1–4, an oracle against Egypt in which YHWH arrives on his cloud chariot and ultimately installs an oppressive king over the people. Isaiah describes this act as judgment on Egyptian counsel and guidance. The Egyptians will consult their אלילים, along with spiritists and mediums, yet those alleged sources of knowledge will fail them, leading to civil war and Assyrian suzerainty. This chapter will explore the ways Isa 19 connects the אלילים to the destruction of Egypt's political wisdom. It also considers ways that Isa 19 functioned rhetorically for a Judean audience, bolstering confidence in YHWH's supreme wisdom. The prophet distinguishes YHWH in terms of his inalterable plans, which stand in contrast to the folly of Egyptian wisdom. The אלילים, in this passage, epitomize the folly of Egyptian counsel and aid. All who deify Egyptian aid become like those who trust the אֱלִילִים. They become אֱוִלִים (fools).

This chapter will begin with a consideration of the literary structure and poetry of Isa 19:1–4 and 11–15, with attention to the role of the אלילים. We will then step back to examine the significance of the wisdom theme in First Isaiah, before returning to Isa 19. I also consider the possibility that Isa 19:3 removes the reference to "gods" from Isa 8:19.

---

1. O'Kane, "Wisdom Influence"; Wildberger, *Isaiah 28–39*, 596–615.
2. On the former, see 28:21; 29:15–16; 31:2. On the latter, see 5:21; 10:13; 19:11–12; 29:14.
3. Isa 6:9–10; 19:14–15; 29:9–10. Discussed in Hayes, "'Spirit of Deep Sleep.'" The flip side of the disruption theme is that of YHWH opening the eyes, ears, and mouth of his people (e.g., 29:18, 24; 32:3).

YHWH's Arrival and the Deluding of Egypt's "Wise" (19:1–4, 11–15)

Isaiah 19 divides into two major sections. The first section (vv. 1–15) begins with the prophetic oracle marker מַשָּׂא—one of ten in First Isaiah—and the second (vv. 16–24) includes a series of five "in that day" oracles.[4] The chapter includes several echoes of the exodus story, most notably the installation of an oppressor over Egypt in v. 4 and the sending of a deliverer in v. 20. The middle section focuses on the confusion of Egypt's political wisdom and the Nile drying up. The chapter also progresses from illicit objects of devotion in vv. 1–4 to YHWH worship in vv. 16–24.

Verses 1–15 focus on the dramatic arrival of YHWH and his unmasking of Egypt's sources of wisdom and power. Verses 1–4 and 11–15 clearly belong together, as the latter completes the action begun in the former.[5] For this reason, I treat them as a pair, even though the latter may be a secondary addition to the earlier vv. 1–4.[6]

Isaiah 19:1–4

Discrediting and unmasking Egyptian wisdom follows YHWH's theophanic arrival in vv. 1–4, where the אלילים appear. Verses 1–4 reflect a movement by YHWH into Egypt in order to destroy their false counsel:

A prophecy about Egypt.

Behold, YHWH, riding upon a swift storm cloud;	[Divine arrival]
and he comes toward Egypt.	
the fraud gods (אלילים) totter before him,	
while the heart of Egypt melts within them.	
I will incite Egyptian against Egyptian;	[Egypt *contra* Egypt]
and they will make war, each against his brother,	
and each against his friend,	
city against city,	
kingdom against kingdom.	
The spirit of the Egyptians will fail within them (בקרבו),	

---

4. 19:16–17, 18, 19–22, 23, 24.
5. See discussion in Blenkinsopp, *Isaiah 1–39*, 315.
6. Cook, *A Sign and a Wonder*, 86–89, considers vv. 11–14 *Fortschreibung*.

> And I will swallow their counsel.   [Destroying false counsel]
> Such that they will consult their fraud deities
>   (אלילים),
> and (their) ghosts of the dead,
> and (their) necromancers,
> and (their) spiritists.
> I will trap Egypt by the power of harsh
>   overlords,
> And a fierce king will rule them.
>   Oracle of the sovereign, YHWH of armies.

The אלילים receive two mentions in this passage. In the first place, the אלילים "totter" before him (v. 1). Then, the Egyptians consult their אלילים in v. 3, but apparently in a state of YHWH-induced delusion. The final two verses (vv. 3–4) suggest a connection between Egypt's confused counsel and their subjugation to cruel masters.

The theophanic arrival of YHWH on a storm cloud is unique within Isaiah, but is also present in the exodus story, and throughout Israel's early poetry (Exod 15:8–10; Judg 5:4–5; Hab 3:3–15). YHWH's arrival on a swift cloud evokes his dramatic appearances in judgment and suggests here that YHWH will appear suddenly, causing widespread fear and confusion. While the image of YHWH arriving on a cloud does not appear elsewhere in Isaiah, his theophanic arrival on a chariot is suggested already in Isa 6. In that scene, Isaiah sees YHWH seated, but as he sees him the temple doorposts quake and the temple itself "fills" with smoke (v. 4). The bold assertion of YHWH's name האדון יהוה צבאות reflects his royal status vis-à-vis the Egyptians in a way that is further analogous to YHWH's exalted royal status in Isa 6. In Isa 19 it is not the prophet, or even Israel, but rather Egypt and its non-gods that tremble before YHWH.

The trembling אלילי מצרים may be a subtle echo of Exod 12:12, where we read that YHWH would enact punishment on all the אלהי מצרים. In Isa 19, however, YHWH's "mere appearance is sufficient to destroy the false gods."[7] Just as the hearts of Canaan's inhabitants melted (Josh 2:11), and in Isaiah the Babylonians' hearts melted (13:7) before YHWH, so the Egyptians' hearts melt and the idols tremble.[8] Presumably, they fall over.

The idea that Egypt's fraud-deities (אלילים) should tremble before YHWH (Isa 19:1) might imply that Isaiah lends them a degree of agency. This is similar to the ostensible problem of idol agency in Isa 2:5–22, where in an earlier

---

[7]. Kaiser, *Isaiah 13–39*, 100.
[8]. In addition, the language of Egypt's heart (לבב) failing at YHWH's arrival echoes Ahaz's and the people's response to the Syro-Ephraimite coalition (Isa 7:2).

form of the passage it seems like the *idols* hide in the cliffs and crevasses of the rocks (v. 21).⁹ However, the verb *נוע seems to describe a theophanic effect, the shaking of the land caused by the arrival of YHWH's presence. The same verb *נוע describes the temple doorposts in Isa 6:4, which quake at YHWH's arrival. Moreover, the image is mocking. It imagines the אלילים wobbling and about to fall as YHWH arrives and, at the same time, trembling in fear before him. Keil and Delitzsch express the point well: "They must shake, for they are to be thrown down; and their shaking for fear is a shaking to their fall."¹⁰ It is also important to bear in mind that the prophet does not seem as particularly focused on their nonexistence as he does on exposing them by any means as frauds, only worthy of mockery, and of denying them any divine status. Moreover, the poetic nature of this description allows for imprecision concerning whether or not fraud deities could, in fact, tremble.

Verses 2–4 outline YHWH's action using three key verbs: "incite," "swallow," and "trap." YHWH would incite civil war in Egypt, swallow their counsel, and trap them under the power of harsh rulers. The prospect of inciting civil war evokes a similar pronouncement of judgment on Judah in Isa 3:5. But now the same principle is applied to Egypt. The circle of strife and chaos radiates outward from brother and neighbor to city and kingdom.

The prophet returns to the אלילים in 19:3 to describe the result of YHWH "swallowing" any wise counsel Egypt might have had. This verse shifts our attention from the trembling of the fraudulent gods—which attacks their credibility—to the folly of the Egyptians consulting them. The language shifts from third to first person in v. 2, which may be explained in redactional terms, or perhaps more likely, in terms of a shift in perspective occasioned by YHWH's arrival, which gives way to first-person speech (vv. 2ff). Verse 3 depicts the Egyptians consulting mediums associated with the cult of the dead.¹¹ Pursuing these avenues of "wisdom" is, unbeknownst to the Egyptians, a doomed endeavor. YHWH has frustrated the wisdom of the Egyptians, once again, and set them against one another. The cult of the dead was truly a dead end.

The Egyptians, confused in their strategy, turn toward dead ends, consulting them at YHWH's behest. The list of four consulted sources (v. 3) is difficult to translate. I have already discussed the meaning of the term אלילים, which leads the list.¹² The meaning of the other three terms in the list from 19:3 bring little agreement among commentators. The word אטים is a *hapax* but may be related to the Akkadian *eṭemmu*, or "ghost of a dead person."¹³ The א[ו]בות are more

---

9. See the redaction critical argument of Williamson, *Isaiah 1–5*, 228.
10. Keil and Delitzsch, *Commentary on the Old Testament*, 7:355.
11. Hays, *Death in the Iron Age II*, 8.
12. This was discussed in ch. 1.
13. CAD E 397–401.

familiar in the Hebrew Bible, perhaps most famously when Saul consults an אשת בעלת־אוב, literally, a "woman (who is) a mistress of a spirit of the dead" (1 Sam 28:7). So, the אוב can refer to the spirit of the dead itself, or in other contexts it functions as a shorthand for one who convenes with the spirit—the necromancer (Deut 18:11; Lev 19:31). In still other situations, the term seems to refer to idols, reflecting a loss of knowledge about its original meaning.[14] The ידענים occupy the last position in this brief list. The title ידענים clearly relates to *ידע ("to know"), but has a more technical meaning of "soothsayer," or "spiritist."

This list of four—fraud deities, ghosts of the dead, necromancers, and spiritists—in 19:3 reflects a concern with the cult of the dead that finds fairly widespread representation in First Isaiah.[15] The pairing of א[ו]בות and ידענים (in singular or plural) is common.[16] They almost never occur alone. They even occur together in Isa 8:23, a text to which we will shortly return. The pairing of four forbidden spiritual sources also occurs on several occasions, suggesting something of a set grouping. 2 Kings 21:6 pairs the practice of "soothsaying and augury" with the "necromancers and spiritists." 2 Kings 23:24 pairs the "necromancers and spiritists" with the "teraphim and idols." Perhaps most importantly, Deut 18:11 pairs the "one who casts spells and necromancer" with the "spiritist" and "inquirer of the dead." The pattern seems to derive from the basic pairing of a category relating to necromancy—either their spirits or those who access the dead—and another relating to divination.

The inclusion of the אלילים in the list is a First Isaian innovation, and never appears alongside other such stock lists in the Pentateuch or elsewhere. Some scholars detect Deuteronomistic influence, because of the idol polemic here and in 19:1.[17] However, if this is so, the choice of terms is decidedly *not* Deuteronomistic.[18]

Verse 4 mentions YHWH "swallowing" (*בלע) the counsel of Egypt. This evocative verb choice appears to be deliberate. It reflects a similar use from Isa 3:12. In that text, the prophet describes an oppressive social order where leaders "swallow," or "confuse," the direction of their paths. Moreover, the verb choice may also reflect its use in the exodus narrative, where *בלע plays an important role in the dramatic unfolding of the contest between YHWH and Pharaoh. In the prelude to the ten "signs" (אתת), Aaron's rod-serpent "swallows" (*בלע) the rod-serpents of Pharaoh's counselors and magicians (7:11). Pharaoh then shrugs his

---

14. It may even refer to a cultic installation (e.g., 2 Kgs 21:6). See the helpful discussion in Wildberger, *Isaiah 1–12*, 371–72; Hoffner, "Second Millennium Antecedents."

15. See Hays, *Covenant with Death*.

16. Lev 19:31; 20:6, 27; Deut 18:11; 1 Sam 28:3; 2 Kgs 21:6; 23:24; 2 Chr 33:6; Isa 8:19.

17. Discussed in Aster, *Reflections*, 115, who cites Marti, *Das Buch Jesaja*, 155; Vermeylen, *Du Prophète Isaïe*, 321; Schipper, "'City by the Sea," 25–46.

18. See discussion of Deuteronomistic influence in ch. 2, pp. 52–55.

shoulders and as with the other ten, he and his counselors fail to read the signs of their own impending doom.[19] Later, Pharaoh's army is "swallowed" (*בלע) by the earth in the Reedy Sea (15:13), fulfilling the initial sign given in 7:11. Isaiah's logic follows a similar sequence. The alleged sources of wisdom fail to provide insight or forewarning. The Egyptians fail to read the signs, and like Pharaoh, YHWH caused their lack of insight in order to expose the foolishness of the wise and bring about Egypt's destruction. Rather than Egypt's plans, it is YHWH's that will come to pass (Isa 19:17). Thus, the claim in v. 3 that YHWH will swallow the counsel of the wise acts as a prophetic sign of their impending doom. Now Egypt would experience a harsh slave master (vv. 4, 20).

The use of אלילים at the beginning of 19:3 with the definite article suggests that the term is fronting the group to foreground the fraudulent nature of Egyptian sources of knowledge. While not necessarily claiming that they are all idols, the term האלילים foregrounds the fact that the Egyptian sources of knowledge are unreliable. They have the appearance of reality but, like the term האלילים itself, are not the real thing. As we see below, they reduce their adherents to אֱוִלִים (fools).

Isaiah 19:11–15

After YHWH arrives (vv. 1–4), the scenery shifts toward the Nile—dry and cracked—with all its dependents mourning and lamenting (vv. 5–10). The placement of vv. 5–10 might have been triggered by the theophanic scene in vv. 1–4. YHWH arrives and the land is laid bare and dry before him. The dry Nile is not otherwise related in any obvious way to the oppressive king placed over the Egyptians in v. 4. As we read later in Isaiah, "By my (i.e., YHWH's) rebuke I dry up the sea, I make the rivers a desert" (Isa 50:2). After describing the total collapse of Egypt's economy and society due to the dry Nile, the prophet turns deftly toward those with power to "do something" (vv. 11–14). As in the exodus story, we wonder if the court counselors can effect good. The counselors attempt wise counsel (עצה, as in v. 4), but offer only folly. Egyptian sages and counselors were notorious and, here, spectacularly confused. The Egyptians cannot even induce the wise to speak (vv. 11–12). They are, in fact, אֱוִלִים (fools), a rare plural form that mimics the vowel pattern of the אֱלִילִים ("fraud gods").[20] The Egyptians become like the idols they trust. Like a drunk offering his drink to other would-be drunks, the counselors make the people of Egypt stagger. It

---

19. Fretheim, "Plagues as Ecological Signs."
20. The plural appears elsewhere in Prov 1:7, 10:21, and Isa 35:8. In Zech 11:15, the rare noun אֱוִלִי appears. *HALOT* (ad loc.) proposes אֱלִיל instead, highlighting the potential for confusion between these terms. Delitzsch proposes אֱוִיל.

turns out that YHWH induced such confusion by unleashing a spirit of "staggering about" (vv. 14–15).²¹

The reference to the "spirit of staggering about" (19:14) like a drunk reoccurs in Isa 28:7–8 and 29:9–10, where it describes *Israel's* counselors, the priests, seers, and prophets. Moreover, the prophet's description of disabling "head and tail" in 19:15 evokes the prophecy that YHWH would cut off Israel's "head and tail" (9:14). These intertexts highlight the degree to which the judgments against Egypt also shines the spotlight on Israel's own corrupt leadership. Notably, the judgments in Isa 19 have little to do with any specific injustice, hubris, or misdeeds against Israel. Instead, the prophet's concern seems to lie in the way that Israel's leadership depended on Egyptian aid, counsel, and support, a common theme in the book. As is often the case, there is an "insider reference" to the "outsider context" of prophetic oracles. Critiquing Egypt highlights Israel's own folly.²²

The redactional history of Isa 19 suggests at least three ways that the oracles in Isa 19:11–15 functioned for an Israelite or Judean audience. First, the prophetic oracles against Egyptian aid were likely joined as a bridge to the anti-Egypt narrative in 20:1–6. The prophet thereby urges Israel to forsake Egyptian help, and narrates Egypt's impending subjugation to Assyria, the "hard master" of 19:4. Second, an editor appended a series of "in that day" (ביום ההוא) oracles in 19:16–25.²³ The first of these (vv. 16–17) predicts Egypt's fear of Judah due to YHWH's terrible plan against them. This oracle casts vv. 11–15 in terms of Judean supremacy over Egypt. Third, the latter series of four oracles (vv. 18–25) envision Assyria, Egypt, and Judah worshiping YHWH. Among the series of reversals these oracles foretell is the sending of a savior to "defend and deliver" Egypt (19:20). This recasts the earlier prophecy against Egypt in terms of a prelude to Egypt's healing (19:22).

The insider referentiality of Isaiah's oracles against Egypt highlight several features of 19:1–15 that pertain to our study of divine supremacy and the folly of the אלילים. First, the prophet epitomizes Israel's "worship" of Egyptian aid in terms of the אלילים who, at the arrival of YHWH do nothing but tremble in fear. We noted how the term אלילים relates to fraudulent sources of knowledge, to which Israel apparently turned in times of trouble (cf. 2:6–8; 8:18–19), and to the fools (אולים) who trust them. YHWH pours confusion over such efforts to "know," such that Egypt becomes subjugated. Second, the prophet also highlights the supremacy of YHWH's wisdom over Egyptian wisdom. Egypt's court officials considered themselves "heirs of their nation's great tradition of wisdom

---

21. Watts, *Isaiah 1–33*, 254.
22. Smith, "Polemic of Biblical Monotheism," 201–34.
23. Blenkinsopp, *Isaiah 1–39*, 313–14.

and as members of ancient royal families."[24] Yet their plans were doomed to failure because of YHWH's superior plan against them. As such, Isaiah highlights the superiority of Israel's prophets over the court officials of Egypt (19:12, 16–17) and, in the process, highlights YHWH's superior wisdom.

The Plans and Wisdom of YHWH

The theme of wise and foolish counsel (from diviners et al.) plays a major role in the book of Isaiah. Scholars have long wrestled with the degree to which Isaiah exhibits speech forms and content from wisdom literature, or whether such similarities are the product of wisdom traditions or schools.[25] For our purposes, the putative origins of such material is less important than the presence of thematic content related to divine wisdom and human foolishness. Specifically, this wisdom or foolishness relates consistently in Isaiah to the ability to discern YHWH's hand in directing world events. Along such lines, several scholars have noted the thematic importance of YHWH's "plans" in the book.[26] YHWH's plans pertain to his actions in Israel and among the nations that those who claim wisdom tend to oppose. The verb *יעץ ("to advise, counsel") and its nominal עצה occur more frequently in Isaiah than in any other Old Testament book (35 of 175 occurrences, or 20 percent).[27] It occurs frequently in the oracles against the nations in Isa 13–23, often to describe divine opposition to the pride of the nations, whose own plans come to nothing.[28] A key emphasis in texts pertaining to YHWH's "plans" is the fact that they triumph over any attempted human plans and that YHWH frustrates plans of those who are "wise in their own eyes" (5:21). YHWH's superior plan constitutes one of the primary ways that First Isaiah distinguishes YHWH in absolute terms.

Within First Isaiah, forms of the verbal root *יעץ cluster in five primary texts. We gain a sense of the thematic significance of the divine plan by looking briefly at each. First, in Isa 7–8, Ahaz lives in fear because Syria and Israel "plotted against" (על + *יעץ) him (7:5). Yet Isaiah insists that this plan will not "stand" (*קום, a verb often associated with plans). As Jacob Stromberg points out, the narrative deliberately names "the house of David" as the object of the nations'

---

24. Kaiser, *Isaiah 13–39*; Schmid, *Wesen und Geschichte der Weisheit*.
25. On wisdom in Isaiah, see Fichtner, "Isaiah Among the Wise," 428–38; Whedbee, *Isaiah and Wisdom*; cf. the extensive bibliography on wisdom in Isaiah in Wilson, "Wisdom in Isaiah," 166–67.
26. Fichtner, "Jahwes Plan"; Albrektson, "Divine Plan"; Brueggemann, "Planned People/Planned Book?" 1:19–37.
27. Jensen, "Yahweh's Plan," 445.
28. Discussed in Balogh, *Stele of YHWH in Egypt*, 280–83. The verb יעץ occurs in 14:24, 26, 27; 23:8, 9; עצה occurs in 14:26 and 16:3. Balogh also notes the synonyms דמה, חשב, and צוה that occur in the oracles against the nations.

"plans" (7:2). It is the "house of David" that would be vindicated in the face of this coalition, which soon gave way to a larger Assyrian threat.[29] "If you (plural) do not believe, you will not be established," the prophet proclaims (7:9). This promise obtains for subsequent Davidic kings. This proves essential for later Isaianic thinking about Hezekiah's trust in YHWH in the face of the Assyrian threat. Isaiah 8:10 raises the issue of Assyria's threat once again: "Plan a plan (עֻצוּ עֵצָה), but it will be frustrated. Speak a word, but it will not come to pass, for God is with us." Here we are told, for the first time, that Assyria's plans against Judah would come to nothing. This oracle proves especially crucial after the word of doom in 8:5–8.[30] The plans of mighty Assyria would remain unrealized, even opposed.

Second, as though picking up the threads left hanging in Isa 8, Isa 14:24–27 continues the prophetic focus on YHWH's plans. In just a few short verses, we read that YHWH has "sworn," "designed," and "planned" (*יעץ 4×, once in nominal form). Accordingly, what he plans "will be," "will come to pass." Indeed, the prophet asks rhetorically, "Who can annul it? . . . Who will turn it back?" The plans relate to the destruction of Assyria, placed somewhat disjunctively here toward the end of an oracle series against Babylon (Isa 13:1–22; 14:3–21). As Brueggemann points out, the location of this oracle against Assyria after the series against Babylon suggests "that the reference to Assyria . . . becomes typological, referring to defiant imperial power."[31] It is a "cipher for all arrogant power which tries to outflank and defy the power of Yahweh, and which cannot finally do so."[32] Isaiah 14:26 suggests that this sort of typological extension was already operative in the oracle. "This is the purpose (הָעֵצָה) that he purposed (*יעץ)," the prophet proclaims, "concerning all the earth." The prophet is concerned most of all with establishing the fact that YHWH planned such events long before their fulfillment. Moreover, none can frustrate his plans, highlighting once again YHWH's incomparability (v. 27). This theme continues into the narrative portions of First Isaiah. During Sennacherib's assault on Jerusalem, YHWH proclaims with confidence: "Have you not heard that I determined it long ago? I planned from days of old what now I bring to pass, that you should make fortified cities crash into heaps of ruins" (37:26 NRSV). The literary placement of 14:23–27, as well as its paradigmatic function, highlight the prophetic certainty that YHWH's plans would prevail over any opposing human plans.

29. Stromberg, *Introduction*, 86
30. Ibid., 87.
31. Brueggemann, "Planned People," 30. While Isa 14 may refer to an Assyrian king (now ruling Babylon), the repeated references to Babylon are likely meant to highlight the fact that both "powers are joined and represent within the stages of human history the selfsame reality of arrogance, which God's kingship is in the process of destroying and will in the end fully succeed as victorious" (Childs, *Isaiah*, 127).
32. Brueggemann, "Planned People," 31.

Third, Isa 19 includes two references to YHWH's plans (19:12, 17). We will return to these below, but I will mention here that the passage contrasts YHWH's plans with the so-called "wise ones" (חכמים) of Egypt. They were unable to discern the geopolitical activity of God through Assyria, despite their claim to royal descent. The combination of על + *יעץ indicates the degree to which YHWH's plans run contrary to the plans advised by Pharaoh's wise counselors, continuing the oppositional tone from Isa 14.

Fourth, Isa 23:1–14 contains an oracle against the Phoenician Tyre and Sidon in the form of a lament (*ילל in vv. 1, 6, 14), or rather, a directive to lament. The poem employs the "limping" 3-2 rhythm used elsewhere in Isaianic laments (cf. 13:6–22; 14:4–20; 15–16).[33] The lament reaches its climax in vv. 8–14, where the prophet reveals that YHWH facilitated the destruction of Tyre and Sidon. After asking who purposed (*יעץ) such destruction against (again, על + *יעץ), the prophet exclaims that "YHWH of hosts has purposed (*יעץ) it, to defile the pride of all beauty, to cut *all* the honored of the earth down to size." One sees here, as in Isaiah 14, an extension of the prophetic critique to *all* the proud in the earth. This lament evokes the critique of "all" who are high and lofty in Isaiah 2:12–17, discussed in chapter 1. In that short poem, the ships of Tarshish symbolize pride (cf. the reference to Tarshish in 23:6, 14). Here their "stronghold is destroyed" (v. 14). The assertion of YHWH's plans here at the end of Isaiah's oracles of the nations forms a natural bookend with the introductory oracle about YHWH's plans at the end of Isaiah 13–14 (14:24–27). The seismic shifts occurring among the nations were the result of YHWH's own political sovereignty.

Fifth, Isa 32:1–8 sounds a different note than the examples listed above. In this passage, the prophet contrasts the king who "will reign in righteousness" (v. 1) with the fool, who "plans (*יעץ) wicked schemes" (v. 7). The noble person "plans/decides" (*יעץ) noble things (v.8). The passage clearly connects to the righteous king of Isa 11, who rules with a "spirit of wisdom . . . and a spirit of counsel (עצה)."[34] These two passages remind the reader that while YHWH's purposes oppose the arrogance of the nations, he also looks to raise up a leader who renders decisions on the basis of justice and righteousness.

From these texts we observe, first, that YHWH's plans are most often directed against arrogant nations. Their arrogance leads them headlong into disaster. The nations' plans are borne of their own pride, and, as such, they "came into collision with God's plan."[35] Second, the plans of YHWH are inscrutable. The rationale, according to the prophet, is that he might nullify the wisdom of the

---

33. Blenkinsopp, *Isaiah 1–39*, 343. For a discussion of the limping *qinah* rhythm in Isaiah, see Couey, *Reading the Poetry*, 61–63.
34. Cf. Isa 9:5 where the coming ruler is called a פלא יועץ "planner of wonders."
35. Von Rad, *Old Testament Theology*, 2:162, quoted in Wildberger, *Isaiah 1–12*, 203.

wise (Isa 29:14).³⁶ The nations' folly and lack of discernment finds expression in their tendency to rely on so-called "wise men" who cannot read the plans of YHWH, revealed uniquely through his prophet(s). Third, several texts in Isa 1–39 tend to extrapolate to "the nations" or "the earth" on the basis of YHWH's plans against specific nations. What YHWH does to counteract the pride of individual nations reveals something of his pattern for the nations as such. Finally, the plans of YHWH are not only oppositional. They also seek realization through a wise Judean king.

I will now draw attention to several key points noted by scholars that pertain to our understanding of Isaiah's critique of the אלילים in Isa 19 and elsewhere. First, in Wildberger's summary of the theme of the divine plan in his commentary on Isa 1–12, he points out that for Isaiah, YHWH's "plan" does not pertain to strict determinism, as though all events that happen were simply foreordained and rendered certain.³⁷ Rather, YHWH's plans relate to his unique works (*פעל). These works are guided by the metaphor of a "ruler." As such, YHWH is the "absolute lord of history, and he alone gives history its shape."³⁸ For Wildberger, the translation "decide" better fits the sense of *יעץ as it operates within the prophet's royal metaphor for YHWH. Rather than events planned in eternity past, he contends that the term relates to YHWH's responses to specific historical events.³⁹

Brueggemann suggests that prophet's focus on YHWH's "counsel" and "plans" can be understood best in terms of a convergence of "a *prophetic*, oracular assertion of 'God's plan' and a *sapiential* notion of 'plan' as a hidden, underlying order of the historical process."⁴⁰ The first "prophetic" or "oracular" concept, pertains to the idea that (a) YHWH's plans and purposes are asserted over the nations such that they will prevail, and (b) they also defy and confound human wisdom. We have seen both concepts at work in the examples above. The strength of Brueggemann's proposal is its insistence that the divine plan is not "autonomous" but rather responsive to real historical circumstances. But in addition, it is inscrutable to human wisdom. This has the added consequence of upending would-be "divine" sources of wisdom.

Wolfgang Werner offers an intricate redaction historical study of the plan of YHWH theme in Isaiah, focusing on the root word יעץ/עצה.⁴¹ Like Wildberger, Werner examines the question whether Isaiah believed that God has a

---

36. Wildberger, *Isaiah 1–12*, 203. This concept anticipates the greater and higher ways and thoughts of YHWH in Isa 55:9.

37. Ibid., 202–4. Wildberger continues his discussion of the theme in *Isaiah 13–27*, 82–86. Cf. Hans Wildberger, "Jesajas Verständnis der Geschichte."

38. Wildberger, *Isaiah 1–12*, 203.

39. Wildberger, *Isaiah 13–27*, 83.

40. Brueggemann, "Planned People," 27.

41. Werner, *Studien*.

preordained plan that guides history. Unlike Wildberger, however, he finds little evidence for such a belief in the words of Isaiah of Jerusalem. For Werner, the texts in First Isaiah that foreground YHWH's plan are likely postexilic redactions.[42] He suggests that Isa 19:1–15 reflects an awareness that YHWH directs the nations but not that he guides them with a preordained plan. It is Deutero-Isaiah, he argues, who introduces the idea of YHWH's preordained plan with greater force (40:12–17; 44:24–28; 46:9–11), though with specific application to the salvation of Israel. This conviction that YHWH controls history proceeds from there throughout other prophetic literature.[43] Isaiah 25:1–5 is a rare exception in First Isaiah, which according to Werner attests to a universal plan of YHWH.[44] Werner's study complicates efforts to ground the idea of YHWH's preformed plans in preexilic texts. He also highlights the degree to which references to a divine plan are situational and not necessarily universal claims. However, Werner neglects the degree to which Isaiah extrapolates from specific plans to the universal (e.g., Isa 14:26; 18:3; 19:2; 23:9). While the planning itself may not be comprehensive—in terms of YHWH having foreordained all things—the implications of his planning are universal. All proud, honored, and wise will be brought low.

Finally, Joseph Jensen, following the earlier studies of Fichtner, Wildberger, and von Rad, explores Isaiah's emphasis on the unopposable plans of YHWH. Like Brueggemann, he observes that YHWH's plans are portrayed as counterintuitive in Isaiah. They involve judgment on Judah, and they run contrary to human wisdom.[45] Moreover, it is only to YHWH that Isaiah attributes any "plans," as such. Following McKane, Jensen notes that "plans" (or "policy" as McKane prefers) require both wisdom and power to put into effect. Isaiah attributes both of these to YHWH alone. Not to "emperors or statesmen" but only to YHWH alone "belong the ambitious vocabulary of wisdom."[46]

Jensen notes that many of the crosscurrents pertaining to YHWH's "plans" run through Isa 19. Whether or not 19:1–4 and 11–14 are from Isaiah of Jerusalem, Jensen maintains that their content accords with material found elsewhere in the book, including material that most scholars consider early.[47] For instance, YHWH will nullify the plans of Egypt just like he nullified the plans of Aram and Israel against Judah (7:5, 7; 8:10; 30:1). Similarly, the assertion that "Pharaoh's wisest advisors" are fools because they did not heed "what YHWH of hosts has planned against Egypt" (19:11–12) echoes similar critiques of Judah's wise

---

42. Ibid., 7–97.
43. Ibid., 101–31.
44. Ibid., 133–46.
45. Jensen, "Yahweh's Plan," 445.
46. Ibid., 447.
47. Exceptions include Werner, *Studien*; Kaiser, *Isaiah 13–39*, 99.

men (5:21; 29:13–16).⁴⁸ It becomes clear in the critique of Tyre in Isa 23 that the plans of YHWH against the nations are the means by which he brings low the proud. Though Egypt's pride is not in view, the type of wisdom YHWH opposes is clearly that of national leaders who take no note of YHWH. For that reason, he opposes "all glory" and brings into disrepute "all the honored of the earth" (23:9).⁴⁹

YHWH's Superior Wisdom

The preceding survey of divine "plans" and wisdom in Isa 1–39 sharpen our analysis of אלילים in Isa 19:1 and 3 and for explaining the terms by which Isaiah distinguishes YHWH as supreme sovereign. To anticipate a key conclusion from what follows, the problem of the אלילים is to be understood within the context of Isaiah's discussion of human folly and divine wisdom. The diviners and sages, along with their would-be gods, are unable to discern major political movements on the horizon or to imagine their own destruction. Indeed, the very term אלילים, related to the singular אליל ("vain," "worthless"), foregrounds the worthless wisdom that the non-gods (and deities of the nations) bestow. They cannot provide "counsel" (עצה) regarding the death dealing enemy that crouches at their adherents' doorstep. In fact, they—like the diviners who endorse them—lead the people of Egypt to become like Judah, a people who "do not know . . . who do not understand" (1:3).

Isaiah 19 thus draws a sharp contrast between Egyptian confusion and YHWH's plans. It is YHWH who has "planned" such trouble, whose plans will stand (19:12), and by whose plans the wise of the nations are reduced to nothing. Isaiah 19's attentiveness to YHWH's plans highlights a theme that recurs with some frequency in First Isaiah, and which gains momentum in Isa 40–55.

The emphasis on YHWH's planning and purposing also brings the critique of Egyptian and other forms of wisdom into sharp relief. The Egyptian diviners were apparently unable to decipher YHWH's plans (19:12), just as the fraud deities were unable to declare them (19:4). Isaiah's critique of Egyptian wisdom and his declaration of YHWH's judgment on the wise carries forward a series of related pronouncements in First Isaiah that denounce those who are "wise in their own eyes" (5:21). The heart of First Isaiah's critique of wisdom seems to be political. The *advisors* of kings are fools, their counsel confused, and their politically directed divinatory arts doomed to failure. Isaiah also takes aim at the so-called wisdom of the *rulers* themselves. He quotes the Assyrian ruler boasting, "By my strength I have done this, and by my wisdom" (10:13a). Later,

---

48. Jensen, "Yahweh's Plan," 449.
49. Ibid.

the prophet announces that the "wisdom of the wise will perish, and the discernment of the discerning will be hidden away" (29:14). The means by which YHWH would remove the wisdom of the wise varies in chs. 1–39. At times, it seems that YHWH would simply cut off the elite. Among those removed from Judah were the "diviner . . . the wise in secret arts, and the shrewd enchanter" (3:2–3). In other cases, YHWH would destroy the foreign powers whose "wise" Judah had trusted (e.g., Isa 29, 31). In other cases, YHWH announces his plans to frustrate the counsel of prophets and diviners both within Judah (e.g., 29:10) and among other nations (Isa 19). In yet other cases, YHWH would harden the hearts of his people so that they would not comprehend the prophetic word (Isa 6:9–10; 28:11–13; 29:9–12; 30:9–10).[50] He would judge them according to their own folly.

The reference to the fraud images (אלילים) in vv. 1 and 3 highlight the doubly foolish nature of Egyptian sources of knowledge, and uses a term already associated in Isaiah with idols. On the one hand, Isaiah claims that what they consider gods are in fact fraud gods, as the term אלילים suggests throughout First Isaiah. But on the other hand, the term אלילים also conjures up a particular oracular sense in this context. As noted earlier, the word is a pluralized form of אליל, which can mean deceitful or worthless, when applied to oracles from God. Jeremiah 14:14 describes the false prophets who "are prophesying false visions, sham divination [וקסם ואליל], and the deceit of their own heart." Jeremiah's critique draws from the Deuteronomic prohibition on divination (קסם; Deut 18:10, 14), which he considered an illicit form of knowledge in contrast to YHWH's designated prophet (Deut 18:15–22). While Isa 19 does not use the term *divination* (קסם), אלילים clearly relates to divinatory acts in v. 3. This suggests that First Isaiah also recognizes the contrast between divine oracles revealed through the prophet and fraudulent oracles derived from divinatory sources. The term אלילים in vv. 1 and 3 is therefore appropriate for capturing the worthlessness of Egyptian sources of knowledge, akin to what Jeremiah states of his opponents.

Because of that worthlessness, YHWH would completely "swallow" (*בלע) Egypt's counsel (עצה) and eventually unleash his own counsel against them (v. 17). This marks an interesting rhetorical twist in the oracle. It transpires that YHWH drives the Egyptians to such folly. He would YHWH would "swallow" their counsel (עצה; 19:3) and empty the "spirit of Egypt" (רוח־מצרים).[51] As a result, the Egyptians would consult their fraud gods (אלילים), shades, necromancers, and spiritists. Eventually, they would be led into the power of a harsh king (19:4). The divine onslaught continues in 19:11–15. There YHWH pours out

---

50. Blenkinsopp, *Isaiah 1–39*, 409. Cf. Isa 30:10–11.
51. The pairing of רוח and עצה, as Hayes points out, suggests "a lack of insight and discernment" ("Spirit of Deep Sleep," 46).

a "spirit of confusion" (רוּחַ עִוְעִים) upon Egypt's counselors and officials. In turn, Egypt's foolish counselors lead the Egyptian people to stumble in their own vomit like a drunk (19:14).

As Katherine Hayes points out, the theme of judgment through delusion that we find here in 19:1–4 and 11–15 recurs throughout First Isaiah.[52] In one instance, YHWH encourages the stupefied, blind, and drunk among Judah to continue in their ways. He deliberately scrambles and confuses their faculties of perception. The prophet declares that YHWH himself has "poured out upon you a Spirit of deep sleep, and closed your eyes (the prophets), and covered your heads (the seers)" (29:10). YHWH has shut down Israel's primary channels of communication with himself, and blocked their ability to understand. In the next oracle, the prophet declares that "the wisdom of their wise shall perish, and the discernment of the discerning shall be hidden" (29:14).[53] The impetus for this divine demolition job on human wisdom is Israel's attempt to "hide counsel (עֵצָה) too deep for YHWH" (29:15). The likely referent is their "counsel" (עֵצָה) with Egypt, described in the next chapter (30:1–2). Isaiah 31 continues the critique of seeking counsel in Egypt. This time Israel is indicted for seeking help in Egypt but not "consulting" (*דרשׁ) YHWH (31:1). The prophet insists that "he too is wise and brings disaster" (31:2), another reference to the strange and surprising work of God against Egypt and through Assyria.[54]

The depiction of the Egyptians lacking knowledge and wisdom constitutes a particularly biting cultural critique. Like Babylon, Egypt was known for its instructional literature. It was the only genre for which they had a designated term—*sbōyet* ("instruction, teaching").[55] This literature, and the elite scribal class that produced it, placed pride of place on wisdom. It was the Egyptian sages who composed the famous *Teaching for King Merikare* and *Instruction of Amenope*, the latter of which clearly informed Israel's own wisdom literature (Prov 22:17–24:22). In addition to instruction from sages, Egypt, like Babylon, relied on an expert class of priestly diviners who discerned the responses of divine images as they processed from and to their temples.[56] In these processions, images answered questions posed by crowds as divine images passed. Both diviner and sage would have been advisors to the king, providing crucial political advice and counsel.

In several places, however, the prophet shows that a proper response to divine wisdom is to discard the אֱלִילִים. We will look briefly at two. First, in

---

52. Ibid.
53. Translation from the NRSV.
54. Though with obvious resonances in later attacks on Egypt.
55. Simpson, *Literature of Ancient Egypt*, 5; Day, "Egyptian Wisdom Literature."
56. Ciraolo and Seidel, *Magic and Divination*; Morenz, *Egyptian Religion*; Cryer, *Divination in Ancient Israel*.

30:22 the prophet describes the people defiling and scattering their gold- and silver-plated "idols" (פסילים) and "images" (מסכה). Like a menstruation cloth, the people would toss their idols aside, declaring, "Be gone!" The scene evokes the examples from Isa 2:20, where the people toss their gold and silver אלילים into caves when YHWH arrives. But in Isa 30, the defiling of idols follows from the people receiving instruction in YHWH's *torah* (v. 21). Defiling idols is the logical consequence of following YHWH's *torah*.

Second, in 31:6–7 Isaiah enjoins his audience to turn back to the one they betrayed. Doing so, he claims, they will "reject" (*מאס) their gold and silver אלילים that their hands made. Rejecting these non-deities, in context, coincides with the people's rejection of Egypt. The prophet reasons that if Egypt is human, and not divine (לא אל), then the objects that characterize their foolish counsel would be cast away. Israel's appeals to Egypt and trust in their sources of wisdom, were akin to idolatry, whether or not the prophet has actual Judean idolatry in mind.[57] In other words, Isaiah draws attention to the deadly act of divinizing Egyptian power and simultaneously highlights the political supremacy of YHWH. To say that Egypt is "not divine" (לא אל) provides a clear political and epistemological environment within which to situate Isaiah's critique of the אלילים. These idols delude and lead their creators and worshipers into political folly and disaster by providing false knowledge. They will "prove useless to save one from the crises for which they were created and invoked."[58]

By Isaiah's reckoning, those who consider themselves wise and turn from YHWH's wisdom to other sources of knowledge share a basic flaw. They fail to acknowledge YHWH and invest others with qualities belonging only to YHWH. The clearest statement to this effect comes in Isa 31:1–3, where Isaiah excoriates the people for going down to Egypt for help. The people apparently sought military aid from Egypt on the assumption that Egypt was wise. YHWH counters with a restatement of his own wisdom, along with his own irrevocable word (31:2). This section of Isaiah carries in it a rich array of intertextual allusions to other portions of First Isaiah, each of which highlight the folly of trusting in other sources of power.[59] Isaiah 31 continues a thread begun in 30:1–5, where Israel looked to Egypt for aid rather than consulting YHWH's "mouth," or "(prophetic) word" (30:2). In 31:2 Isaiah reminds his audience that "the Egyptians are human, and not divine (ולא אל); their horses are flesh and not spirit." The juxtaposition of the human Egypt to the divine (YHWH) implies that for Isaiah, the appeal to Egypt constituted a divinization of Egypt and its military, symbolized here by its horses. The link between the fraud-gods and military might has already been suggested in Isa 2:7–8, where the gold and silver idols on the one

---

57. On which, see Roberts, *First Isaiah*, 405.
58. Ibid.
59. Wildberger, *Isaiah 28–39*, 208.

hand and chariots and horses on the other come in for prophetic censure. As Brueggemann notes, both denote modes of acquiring security, whether through political protection, knowledge of the future, or economic power.⁶⁰

In sum, within this matrix of authorized versus illegitimate knowledge, the term אלילים in Isa 19:1–3 plays an important role. First, Isa 19:3 uses אלילים to foreground the folly of consulting but YHWH for aid from or knowledge about impending disaster. The term carries an epistemological critique. While the people thought that the necromancers, diviners, spiritists, and indeed deities provided reliable sources of knowledge, they could only yield the incoherent babble of drunks.⁶¹ The אֱלִילִים presage the possibility of becoming אֱוִלִים. Second, the only reliable knowledge came—much to the shame of Egyptian wise men—via the *plans* of "YHWH of armies" (v. 12). Instead of the council declared by Egyptian sages, the "purpose" (עצה) that YHWH "purposes" (*יעץ) against Egypt would come to pass (Isa 19:17).⁶² This would prove disastrous for Israel, who had put stock in Egypt.

Does Isaiah 19:3 Remove the Gods from Isaiah 8:19?

Given the prophet's use of אלילים as an epistemological critique of divinized foreign aid, it remains to be seen if the use in Isa 19:3 also constitutes a deliberate attempt to avoid (or remove) reference to the אלהים. I will represent Isa 8:19–21 here in full for the sake of the subsequent discussion: "And if they say to you, 'Consult the spirits of the dead and the soothsayers who chirp and mutter. Shouldn't a people consult their gods (אלהיו)? *Shouldn't they consult the dead on behalf of the living?*' (Go) to the instruction and testimony! If not, they speak according to *this* word. Then there is no (light of) dawn in them. They will pass by parched and hungry. It will come about that when they become hungry, they will become angry and curse by their king and their gods (ובאלהיו), with faces lifted upward."⁶³ Isaiah 8:19–21 forms part of a larger section of text focused on judging diviners and necromancers and is linked to the previous section (8:16–18) by means of the catchwords "instruction" (תורה) and "testimony" (תעודה).⁶⁴ In that previous section, Isaiah binds up his prophetic testimony and instruction with his disciples (v. 16). The precise nature of this "binding up"

---

60. Brueggemann, *Isaiah 1–39*, 251.
61. Cf. the "wonderful counselor" of Isa 9:6.
62. Notice the use of "YHWH of armies" in vv. 12 and 17, as well as the reuse of the verb *יעץ in both verses.
63. I have supplied words in italic type for clarity.
64. Roberts, *First Isaiah*, 141. The term תעודה occurs only in 8:16 and 20 in the book of Isaiah. The term תורה consistently describes the prophetic word in Isaiah (1:10; 2:3; 5:24; 30:9).

(*צוּר) is unclear. It could be verbal or written in form.[65] Whichever it might be, the implication is that Isaiah's words for and against Judah would eventually be vindicated. The reuse of the terms *instruction* and *testimony* in v. 20 suggests a meaning similar to the earlier use. The people of Judah wanted to consult the dead, and were rejecting the prophetic word. The prophet's injunction, "(Go) to the instruction and testimony!" reflects his exasperation with the people's failure to consult true and acceptable channels of knowledge. Rather than consulting the prophets, the people turn toward the dead and end up cursing by their king and gods. Their refusal to heed that instruction and testimony leaves them wandering in darkness, a point not lost on the author of Isa 29. There, Isaiah returns to this theme to describe those who consult the dead. In the end, he declares, they become like the dead spirits they pursue (29:4). Their "voice will come like a spirit from the ground" (והיה כאוב מארץ קולך).

Comparing Isaiah 8:19 and 19:3

The theme of consulting illicit sources of knowledge in Isa 8:19–21 has obvious resonances with Isa 19:1–4, though the opponents have changed. We have moved from the Judean focus of chs. 7–12 to the international focus of chs. 13–23.[66] Below, I list several key similarities between 8:19 and 19:3.

Isaiah 8:19	Isaiah 19:3
וְכִי־יֹאמְרוּ אֲלֵיכֶם דִּרְשׁוּ אֶל־הָאֹבוֹת וְאֶל־הַיִּדְּעֹנִים הַמְצַפְצְפִים וְהַמַּהְגִּים הֲלוֹא־עַם אֶל־אֱלֹהָיו יִדְרֹשׁ בְּעַד הַחַיִּים אֶל־הַמֵּתִים׃	וְנָבְקָה רוּחַ־מִצְרַיִם בְּקִרְבּוֹ וַעֲצָתוֹ אֲבַלֵּעַ וְדָרְשׁוּ אֶל־הָאֱלִילִים וְאֶל־הָאִטִּים וְאֶל־הָאֹבוֹת וְאֶל־הַיִּדְּעֹנִים׃

Both verses include the familiar pair אבות (necromancers/spirits of the dead) and ידענים (spiritists), and two others. Most notable for our purposes is the occurrence of אלילים in this list. In the Pentateuch, idols never occur in lists pertaining to divination or necromancy.[67] Kings and Chronicles link the practice of necromancy to idolatry,[68] but neither mentions other אלהים. Only Isa 8:19 uses the term אלהים in conjunction with such practices, suggesting that Isa 19 is either drawing on this text, is influenced by this text, or is representing illicit behavior using a shared pattern of representation.

---

65. Wildberger, *Isaiah 1–12*, 366; Roberts, *First Isaiah*, 139; Blenkinsopp, *Isaiah 1–39*, 244; Williamson, *Isaiah 6–12*, 330.
66. With notable exceptions, of course, including 14:1–2.
67. Lev 19:31; 20:6, 27; Deut 18:10–12.
68. 2 Kgs 21:6 (cf. 2 Chr 33:7); 23:24.

The relationship between Isa 8:19 and 19:3 is important for the present study, since the former uses the term אלהים and the latter אלילים. This poses several interesting possibilities for this study. First, if 19:3 echoes 8:19 but substitutes אלילים, then we have further evidence that Isaiah is deliberately substituting the term אלילים for אלהים. The idea that Isaiah would substitute אלילים for אלהים has been suggested already in previous discussions.

To begin, we will look at the possibility of an intertextual link between 8:19 and 19:3. Paul Cook suggests the possibility of "intertextual influence between Isaiah 19:3 and 8:19," although he considers direct influence unlikely. His rationale for excluding direct influence is that the pairing of אבות and ידענים are too common to warrant a special relationship between these texts. Together, they form an "idiomatic expression," and nothing else.[69] That they form an idiomatic expression is undoubtedly true but does not rule out the possibility of a more direct connection between these texts.[70] To sustain any claim of direct or even indirect influence on 19:3 we might consider evidence beyond the two shared terms אבות and ידענים. They are certainly a stock pair that appear occasionally throughout the Hebrew Bible.[71] However, the evidence for an intertextual relationship between 8:19 and 19:3 does not end there.

First, unlike other occurrences, 8:19 and 19:3 use the verb *דרש ("to consult") and list four objects of illicit consultation, suggesting a similar pattern. Biblical authors more commonly use *פנה ("to turn aside") or *עשה ("to use") to describe actions toward prohibited divinatory or necromantic sources. Deuteronomy 18:11 is the only other text that pairs the verb *דרש with these illicit objects, but that Deuteronomic text likely forms part of the background to Isa 8:19.[72] Second, of the texts describing the illicit consultation of the dead, only Deut 18:11, Isa 8:19, and Isa 19:3 use דרש* + אל.[73] Third, 8:19 and 19:4 list two pairs of two prohibited forms of divination. The similarities between these texts suggest that the author of Isa 19 was at least aware of an idiomatic grouping of four like what we see in 8:19 when composing 19:3.[74]

---

69. Cook, *A Sign and a Wonder*, 85.
70. Kaiser, by contrast, suggests that 19:3 is crafted with knowledge of 8:19, but he does so on the assumption that the prophet's critique could not have come from knowledge of actual practices (*Isaiah 13–39*, 101). Brian Schmidt argues similarly that 19:1–15 could not have come from Isaiah since Egypt did not practice necromancy (*Israel's Beneficent Dead*, 154–58). This latter charge can now be dismissed in the light of knowledge about necromancy in Egypt (Hays, *Death in the Iron Age II*, 57–91).
71. Lev 19:31; 20:6, 27; Deut 18:11; 1 Sam 28:3, 9; 2 Kgs 21:6; 23:24; 2 Chr 33:6; Isa 8:19; 19:3.
72. Williamson, *Isaiah 6–12*, 331–35.
73. Ibid., 332.
74. A fourth option for a relationship between these two texts may come from a look at the LXX of Isa 19:3, in which we see τοὺς θεοὺς αὐτῶν. This translation may suggest an underlying Hebrew version with אלהיהם ("their gods"). If we look at translations of האלילים throughout the LXX, we see that θεός is never used, making 19:3 unusual. The use of θεός in 19:3 in close proximity to τὰ

While inconclusive, a literary connection between these two texts is plausible. Determining the direction of influence, if it exists, is difficult to say the least. Commentators will argue variously for one passage or another preceding the other. What is important for our study is to acknowledge that the use of אלהים in 8:19 is unusual for First Isaiah, that 19:3 is closely related, and that 19:3 uses אלילים instead, as is more common throughout First Isaiah.

Several additional points deserve mention regarding Isa 8:19 (and v. 21). First, it is important that the reference to אלהים in v. 19 seems to be in the mouth of Isaiah's opponents, and not on the prophet's own lips. The reference to אלהים in v. 21 depends rhetorically on that quoted portion in v. 19 and for this reason may follow suit. Second, Isa 8:19–21 clearly echoes Deut 18:11–20. Both passages use the terms ידעים and אוב and prohibit consulting the dead using the construction *דרש + object. Moreover, both passages contrast listening to spiritists and diviners rather than the word of YHWH through his prophet.[75] Given these similarities, we might suggest that אלהים in Isa 8:19 *and* 21 depend on Deuteronomy's use in 18:20. Deuteronomy contrasts those who listen to the true prophet with those who listen to "other gods" (Deut 18:20).

Third, it is also worth noting that syntactically, both 8:19 and 21 might refer to YHWH and *not* other deities, though contextually this is unlikely. The LXX goes this direction. It translates אלהים with the singular θεός in v. 19, bringing the direct quotation of Isaiah's opponents to an earlier conclusion: "And if people say to you, 'Seek those who utter sounds from the earth and the ventriloquists, the babblers who utter sounds out of their bellies,' should not a nation be with its God (θεὸν αὐτοῦ)? Why do they seek out the dead concerning the living?"[76] The LXX lacks any reference to god(s) in v. 21 and instead follows a literal rendering of the Aramaic פתכרא (τὰ παταχρα, "idols").[77] Similarly, the Isaiah Targum, has פתכר ("idol") and טעו ("idol") for אלהים in vv. 19 and 21.

Other traditions preserve the term's divine connotations but suggest that YHWH is the referent. 1QIsa\u1d43 and the Vulgate also render אלהים in vv. 19 and 21 as singular referents. This tradition of translating 8:19 and 21 in ways that refer to YHWH continues into English translations like the KJV: "should not a people

---

χειροποίητα (the handmade things; 19:1) is unusual and may reflect an underlying Hebrew variant. However, the Vulgate's *simulacra* (images/idols) and the Targum's עֲוָן (idols) reflect no extant variant tradition. One possibility for this anomalous use of θεός in LXX 19:3 is that the writer was familiar with Isa 8:19 and supplied a "memory variant," that is, a textual variant wrought by copying via text-aided memory. Isaiah 8:19 is the only other text in First Isaiah that uses θεός in reference to another deity. In other words, a Greek (or Hebrew) scribe may have mentally associated אלילים with אלהים when translating (or transmitting) the text, leading to a vocabulary shift or harmonization terms from other texts. Of course, other options are available to explain the underlying θεός.

75. Williamson, *Isaiah 6–12*, 332.
76. NETS translation.
77. LXX Isa 37:38 likewise translates אלהיו as τὸν παταχρον αὐτοῦ (his idol).

seek unto their God?" (KJV). In fact, until recent times, translators have tended to prefer a singular translation of אלהים in vv. 19 and 21, though the plural option "gods/idols" never died out.[78]

Reading Isaiah 8:19 and 19:3 Together

Having considered the Deuteronomic background to Isa 8:19 and the literary and semantic basis for the relationship between Isa 8:19 and 19:3, we turn now to consider the effect of reading these texts together. To do so, we will consider the literary and rhetorical context of Isa 19, with due consideration of 8:19 and 21. As noted above, Isaiah's concern is not simply with the mere (mental) divinization of Egypt. Isaiah was not only critiquing the people's estimation of Egypt as a supremely powerful source of help. He was also critiquing the *appeal* to Egyptian support and the concomitant refusal to "seek" (*דרש*) YHWH. In other words, his critique was epistemological, about legitimate and illegitimate sources of knowledge about things to come. The prophet is concerned with the prospect of the people treating Egypt as possessor of viable sources of knowledge. In bypassing YHWH for Egypt, the people neglected YHWH's superior wisdom.

In this regard, the occurrence of אלילים + *דרש* (consult + deity) is most relevant. For Isaiah, consulting diviners and spiritists was akin to abandoning YHWH, who speaks exclusively through his representative prophets about coming geopolitical events.[79] In 19:3, of course, the concern is not that the Egyptians were disobeying YHWH's word. They were not beholden to Israel's laws concerning idols or divination. There is no hint in the text that YHWH's judgment on Egypt was because of its worship of other deities.[80] Rather, the prophet's rhetorical goal was likely to discredit the very sources of knowledge that Israel sought or held in esteem. We can see from other passages in Isaiah that the prophet was particularly exercised about Israel's repeated appeals to Egyptian political aid and refuge. The latter part of Isa 19 continues with this concern in mind, highlighting the folly and stupidity of Egypt's counselors (19:11–13). All of this sets the stage for the prophet's dramatic enactment of Egypt's impending conquest by the Assyrians in Isa 20. They were the oppressive master about which the prophet warned in Isa 19. With this invasion, the hopes of Israel turn

---

78. Among the reformers, the variety of translations of אלהים continues. The Geneva Study Bible (1599 ed.) translates ובאלהיו in v. 21 as "and his gods," obviously referring to pagan deities. The Luther Bible (1545 ed.) also renders אלהים in v. 21 as the plural: "Wenn sie aber Hunger leiden / werden sie zörnen vnd fluchen jrem Könige vnd jrem Gotte."

79. Cf. Isa 30:1 where the prophet utters a woe oracle against those who "take counsel, but not from me [YHWH]."

80. Contrast, for instance, the critique of Moab for worshiping other deities in Jer 48.

to shame and disgrace (20:5–6). By announcing YHWH's plan to frustrate Egyptian divination, we see the prophet trying to steer his people away from deadly waters. Egyptian counsel was sheer folly and would only lead Israel to its own death and shame. Isaiah will later pronounce "woes" upon those who "go down to Egypt" for help without "consulting" YHWH (30:2; 31:1). "[YHWH] is also wise," the prophet understates.

Conclusions

This study of Isa 19 yields several conclusions that I will rehearse here. First, Isa 19:1–15 constitutes one of the many attacks on the "wise" that appear throughout chs. 1–39. YHWH confuses the wisdom of the wise by pouring out a "spirit of confusion," which has the Egyptians running right into the arms of the אלילים and other useless sources of knowledge. I suggested that the prophet's twofold reference to אלילים highlights the sheer folly of Egyptian help. That which seems to be divine is in fact fraudulent, and those who follow them become אולים ("fools"). Second, the prophet distinguishes YHWH in terms of his superior and unopposable plans and wisdom. His plans and purposes delude and destroy the enemy, and for this reason, his plans should form the basis for Judean confidence in YHWH alone. Third, the prophet's critique on the אלילים is not a purely "religious" matter. It was also political and epistemological. He critiqued the *appeal* to Egyptian support and the concomitant refusal to "seek" (דרש*) YHWH. This locates his rhetoric in the battle between legitimate and illegitimate sources of knowledge about things to come. The prophet is concerned with the people treating Egypt as possessor of viable sources of knowledge. In bypassing YHWH as they sought Egypt, the people neglected YHWH's wisdom.

CHAPTER 5

Conclusions and Comparison

THIS SHORT BOOK ARGUES THAT in First Isaiah YHWH's supreme exaltation as sovereign Lord renders laughable the notion of other "gods." They are mocked and simultaneously disappear as אלילים—non-gods. This particular mode of monotheizing is unique to First Isaiah, and takes on a specific form in the book's first 35 chapters. It therefore deserves its own place at the table of scholarly discussion about monotheistic rhetoric in the Old Testament. While some scholars have observed the book's monotheistic perspective, the uniqueness of the book's monotheistic rhetoric about the non-deities has not been previously detailed.

To this end, this book advanced several arguments, focusing on key texts where the First Isaian neologism אלילים appears. This term is used rhetorically by Isaiah to emphasize three things: (1) unreliability—the אלילים cannot be trusted to deliver what they promise, including reliable knowledge; (2) fraudulence—the אלילים are not what they appear to be; and (3) foolishness—the אֱלִילִים render their devotees אֱוִלִים (fools). This term occurs in close connection with metaphorical expressions of YHWH's exalted status "up high." In Isaiah, a SUPREMACY AS HEIGHT metaphor highlights the fact that being up high is an utterly exclusive status. The metaphor asks us to perceive a world in which supreme power is expressed in vertical terms. Especially after 2:12–17, the root metaphor asks us to *expect* conflict anytime someone other than YHWH takes to the heights. We are also invited to expect that the אלילים, whose very name resembles אלהים, should be cast down to the lowest places when they encounter the true אלהים. It is in these ways that First Isaiah monotheizes.

In ch. 2, I examined the controlling role that Isa 2:6–22 plays in the book. Through interwoven prose and poetic fragments, the passage links the vertical elevation of YHWH with the descent of non-deities into the ground. Not only is the spatial rhetoric about YHWH's exaltation extreme—emphasizing with thunderous force that YHWH opposes *all* that is lifted high—but it also becomes linked by the poet to the forsaking of images *as fraud deities*. I suggested that the monotheistic rhetoric of First Isaiah differs from the language of Second Isaiah. This is also borne out by a semantic comparison between the two literary corpora, represented in appendix 1. And while some affinities exist between First Isaiah's idol polemic and Deuteronomistic language, the similarities cannot be explained in terms of straightforward influence or borrowing. Nor does Second Isaian influence account for the mode of monotheizing in First Isaiah. Instead, First Isaiah develops its own monotheistic discourse. We see examples of how Isa 2:6–22 influences, or is shaped by, such discourse in 17:8 and 31:7.

Chapter 3 examined the use of אלילים in Isa 10. This too is a key chapter in the book of Isaiah, for in it Assyrian destruction comes under explicit condemnation for the first time. Assyria oversteps its remit, and wrongly equates YHWH with the non-deities of the nations. According to the prophet, it is Assyria itself who becomes like the idols, an object of wood that YHWH can wield according to his wishes. I suggested that Isa 10:9–11 borrow material from Isa 36–37, but intentionally remove references to the אלהים, thus highlighting the aversion to the term that we find throughout chs. 1–35. While the gods fade into the background, Isa 10 simultaneously foregrounds YHWH's political supremacy as "the sovereign" (האדון; Isa 10:16, 33).

Finally, ch. 4 examined the use of אלילים in Isa 19. The deployment of the term אלילים highlights an epistemological critique latent in the term itself. Alternative sources of knowledge were considered pure folly, a reality emphasized by the vacuous and worthless אלילים. The term applies to Egyptian images but was also chosen to evoke the range of necromancers, diviners, spiritists, and advisors in whom the Egyptians took pride, and some Judeans apparently held in high esteem. By contrast, YHWH's plans were steadfast and sure. I also suggested that Isa 19:3 may rewrite 8:19 in an effort to remove references to the אלהים. This suggests at least two cases in First Isaiah where a writer in First Isaiah reworks his source to remove the אלהים (discussed in chs. 2–3).

Throughout the study, I also noted at least five occasions where First Isaian language quotes or echoes other passages, but in ways that substitute non-divinizing language for the אלהים found in the quoted or echoed text. For instance, Isa 2:5 seems to omit the reference to the nations' gods in Mic 2:5b deliberately. Isaiah 10:10–11 draws from Isa 36:19–20 but substitutes אלילים for the אלהים. Isaiah 19:1 may allude to Exod 12:12 and substitute a reference to Egyptian אלילים for the Egyptian אלהים. Isaiah 19:3 seems to draw from Isa 8:19 but omits its reference to אלהים. Finally, Isa 26:13 substitutes (human) אדנים for the אלהים used elsewhere. This range of substitutions supports my thesis that in First Isaiah the gods disappear.

Having considered First Isaiah's discourse about the non-gods, I will now step back to consider the relationship between monotheistic discourse in First and Second Isaiah. I suggest that while First and Second Isaian influence the other's monotheistic discourse, that influence is minor. This is *despite* the evidence that Second Isaiah (and to some extent Third Isaiah) played a role in the redaction of First Isaiah.[1] That redactional activity did not necessarily conform the book's theological rhetoric to that of Second Isaiah. Nevertheless, there are thematic resonances (some rooted in semantic links) that highlight a shared concern to distinguish YHWH in absolute terms, and by analogous means. I begin

---

1. Williamson, *Book Called Isaiah*.

Deutero-Isaiah and Monotheism

One of the more perplexing issues facing this study is why the אלילים are absent from Deutero-Isaiah, and why some of Deutero-Isaiah's prominent assertions of YHWH's supremacy are missing from First Isaiah. We have already addressed some of the differences above, and appendix 1 highlights the substantial terminological differences for illicit objects of cultic devotion. Appendix 2 details differences in terminology related to YHWH's exaltation. This would be unremarkable were it not also the case that First and Second Isaiah seem to influence each other's development.[2] Why would the central expression of YHWH's transcendent uniqueness achieve some level of consistency across the book? This question deserves some reflection here in the conclusion. Explaining absences will involve some conjecture, and a short detour into Deutero-Isaiah's mode of monotheizing. This will help set the stage for my considerations of how the two bodies of literature generally part ways regarding the mode of expressing YHWH's sole divinity, yet come to analogous conclusions.

Deutero-Isaiah concentrates most of its monotheizing rhetoric in chs. 43–48. This suggests that monotheizing was more of a rhetorical "moment" than a new religious stage.[3] Deutero-Isaiah addresses specific concerns raised by the exiles about YHWH's ability to know the future or save his people from their plight.[4] To that extent, Deutero-Isaiah's monotheistic rhetoric needs to be situated contextually. Consider the phrase "I am, and there is no other" (אני ואין עוד; Isa 45:5, 6, 18, 21, 22). Babylon also claims, "I am, and there is none else" אני ואפס עוד (Isa 47:8, 10), which echoes the words of Nineveh found elsewhere: אני ואפסי עוד (Zeph 2:15). These rival political assertions, which YHWH counters, pertain to Babylon's imminent downfall and YHWH's deliverance of his people. It is an expression of unrivaled power and not a statement about ontology. These resonances between YHWH's and Babylon's claims suggest that the phrase "I am and there is no other" reflects a particular historical situation in which rival political claims about the governance of history were made by major powers.

In addition, YHWH's sole existence claims belong within a broader rhetoric of negation in which Deutero-Isaiah engages with some frequency. When disputing

---

2. Ibid.; Jeppesen, "Cornerstone"; Lee, *Redactional Study*.
3. For an extensive theological appendix in which he suggests that Deutero-Isaiah and monotheism constitute a new religious stage in Israel, see Wildberger, *Isaiah 28–39*.
4. For a concise summary of Deutero-Isaiah's key themes and arguments, see Stuhlmueller, "Deutero-Isaiah," 8.

the idols' ability to discern the future (Isa 41:21–29), the prophet unleashes a barrage of invectives against their powerlessness over the future. Their inability to speak about what is to come means that they are nothing (מאין; v. 24), and their deeds nothing (מאפע; v. 24). None of the idols could declare (אין מגיד; v. 26) or make known (אין משמיע; v. 28) the future. There was "no counselor" (אין יועץ; v. 28). These negation clauses all pertain to who knows, or does not know, what is to come. Because they do not know, the nations are "frauds" (און), their deeds "nothing" (אפס), and their images "wind" (רוח) and "unformed" (תהו; v. 29). We might call this *oracular impotence*. The nations' gods, and by extension their diviners and makers, cannot know what YHWH has planned—namely, the downfall of Babylon and Israel's deliverance by Cyrus. Isaiah 41:23 challenges the idols to declare the past or future "so that we may know that you are gods." Failing that epistemological litmus test, Deutero-Isaiah finds their claims to divinity wanting. By contrast, YHWH alone knows the past and future. Here, Goldingay says, "The distinctive thing about deity as represented in YHWH's person is the capacity to give an account of history past and future."[5]

Deutero-Isaiah also insists that only YHWH can deliver Israel from exile. Continuing the rhetoric of negation, we hear, "I, I am YHWH, and there is no savior but me" (אנכי אנכי יהוה ואין מבלעדי מושיע; 43:11). The prophet continues in v. 13, stating that "there is none who can deliver from my hand" (ואין מיד מציל). The emphasis on YHWH's exclusive ability to save (via Cyrus) helps situate other claims that YHWH is, "and there is no other God" (43:10; 44:6; cf. 45:5). The title "God," or deity (אל/אלהים), is defined in terms of an exclusive soteriological claim. As MacDonald notes, "The monotheism of Second Isaiah is soteriologically, not ontologically, orientated."[6] In other words, Deutero-Isaiah highlights the gods' and nations' *salvific impotence*. Trito-Isaiah continues along similar lines: "From ancient times none has heard, and none has perceived, no eye has seen a God except you, who acts for those who wait for him" (64:3).

In sum, Deutero-Isaiah foregrounds YHWH's exclusive political sovereignty, exclusive knowledge of the future, and his exclusive ability to save. The phrase "I am, and there is no other" makes best sense with reference to these particular political, epistemological, and soteriological anxieties that beset the exiles (expressed in Deutero-Isaiah's disputation oracles).[7] Deutero-Isaiah was not interested in an abstract discussion about divine existence but in YHWH's monarchy, mono-agency (his ability to save), and mono-mastery of all things past and future. Each pertains to the specific circumstances facing Israel in exile.

This contextual specificity deserves serious consideration when reflecting on the relative lack of Deutero-Isaian influence on First Isaiah's monotheism.

---

5. Goldingay and Payne, *Isaiah 40–55*, 339 (cf. p. 197).

6. MacDonald, "Monotheism and Isaiah," 59. See also Smith, "Polemic of Biblical Monotheism," 201–34.

7. On Deutero-Isaiah's disputation oracles, see Melugin, *Formation of Isaiah 40–55*, 28–44.

Specifically, Deutero-Isaiah's claims about YHWH's mono-agency and exclusive control over the future belong squarely within the set of concerns that occupied the exiles. On the whole, Proto- and Deutero-Isaiah address different historical circumstances (with some overlap). Each body of work bears distinctive Assyrian and Babylonian imprints that shape the kind of discourse they attract, even if they attract redactional activity that continued well beyond their originating contexts of production. If, I as just argued, the statement "I am, and there is no other" belongs to the specific soteriological concerns of the exiles, and is limited already to Isa 40–48, it is eminently possible that later redactors understood this.

Second, we might also consider by comparison the lack of influence of Deutero-Isaiah's monotheistic rhetoric on Isa 49–55 and on Trito-Isaiah. With the exception of 64:3, there is very little that advances the theme of YHWH's sole divinity even though it holds such a place of prominence in Deutero-Isaiah.[8] One may assume here that the mutually influencing redactional activity that undoubtedly stitched the book together nevertheless preserved some of the distinctive theological "modes of monotheizing" present in each. Redactional activity did not erase difference.

Third, some of the aforementioned differences, especially those pertaining to idols, likely reflect the different geographical settings of First and Second Isaiah. In his comparative study of idol language in Proto and Deutero-Isaiah, Williamson notes that the two works reflect different idol types, dates, and geographical settings. The language for "idol," or if we expand this group to include illicit objects of devotion and cultic activity, differs markedly between First and Second Isaiah, as shown in appendix 1. Williamson notes that while First Isaiah focuses on idols *within Yahwistic religion*, Second Isaiah addresses *Babylonian idols*.[9] These differences reflect their differing Judean and Babylonian settings. With the exception of Isa 19, in which the collapse of Egyptian idols prepares the way for Yahwistic altars, this point generally holds. Whether we can explain those differences in terms of differing dates is open for debate. Williamson is confident that texts relating to the אלילים are all late additions that postdate Deutero-Isaiah. This may be the case, but I see little conclusive evidence. While some, if not most, of the אלילים texts are secondary, that does little to help us date them. Other biblical references to the אלילים do seem later (e.g., Lev 19:4; 26:1; Ps 96:5; 97:7), but they might be drawing from an earlier First Isaian tradition. None of those other texts suggest a clear direction of influence, and it seems more likely that First Isaiah is the originator of the term that others adopt. And while the final form of each portion of Isaiah reflects exilic and postexilic concerns, it seems that each also maintained its focus on Judean (FI) and Babylonian (DI) idolatry respectively.

---

8. On the role of Trito-Isaiah in the book's formation, see Stromberg, *Isaiah After Exile*.
9. Williamson, "Idols in Isaiah," 25–26.

Finally, it seems likely that concerns other than YHWH's sole divinity drove the shaping of Isaiah's final form. For instance, the hope of a return from exile and the complete transformation of the people and land structures the final form of First Isaiah and the book as a whole. Webb points out that the final form of Isaiah reflects a concern over threats to Zion, whose status and future is in jeopardy. The solution, he observes, is the "emergence and eventual perfection of a faithful remnant." Thus at the conclusion of chs. 1–12, 24–27, 28–35, 36–39, 40–55, and 56–66 we witness a remnant returning to Zion with singing and worshipping.[10] Themes such as blindness and deafness, the election of Israel, and the "former" and "latter" things also unify the book, and may simply reflect Deutero-Isaiah continuing the themes of Proto-Isaiah or vice versa.[11]

But even a detailed look at any specific example just listed will see development and differences in those themes across the book. As an example, several studies have observed the importance of "justice" throughout Isaiah, but note its different sense and meaning in the book's major sections.[12] In any case, it appears that the specific phrases typically associated with *monotheism* in Deutero-Isaiah exerted little influence on chs. 1–39. As I suggest below, there are certainly key terms that recur across the two corpora, and which bind the theology of Proto and Deutero-Isaiah together, but we are on firmer ground by talking about *analogous modes of monotheizing* rather than direct influence one way or another.[13] If we take monotheizing as a theological tendency in the book, we witness diverse modes of monotheizing across Isaiah.

The relative absence of Deutero-Isaian monotheistic formulations in Proto-Isaiah, and vice versa, is only surprising if one assumes that mutual influence was pervasive and theologically comprehensive. If, however, such influence was strategic and concentrated, then the retention of distinctive modes of monotheizing in both bodies of literature makes sense. Some anti-idol texts reflect possible Deutero-Isaian influence. For instance, the exclamation "Fallen, fallen is Babylon, and all the images of her gods (פסילי אלהיה) are smashed on the ground" (21:9) might indicate that Deutero-Isaian idol polemic against Babylonian deities influenced First Isaiah.[14] However, others point out that the Babylonian images were not destroyed by Cyrus, and that Isaiah 21:9 reflects Sennacherib's much earlier campaign against the city in 689 BCE.[15] Alternatively,

---

10. Webb, "Zion in Transformation"; Stromberg, *Introduction*, 24–25.
11. For the former view, see Clements, "Beyond Tradition-History."
12. Rendtorff, "Zur Komposition."
13. For further studies on the thematic connections between First and Second Isaiah, see Clements, "Beyond Tradition-History"; Seitz, "Divine Council."
14. Duhm, *Das Buch Jesaia*, 121, suggested that this text came from the time of Cyrus, though he does not attribute 21:1–10 to Deutero-Isaiah. Instead, Duhm argues that 21:1–15 come from another late exilic/postexilic author who lived in Palestine (*Israels Propheten*, 285–91).
15. See the summary in Roberts, *First Isaiah*, 274–75.

the prophet might be speaking hyperbolically, as Duhm suggested long ago.[16] In my opinion, the most likely option is that such ways of construing the coming desolation of Babylon were simply prevalent in late exilic/early postexilic texts. Jer 51:8 might constitute a literary influence, as might the combination of פסיל + אלהים in Deut 12:3, or any of the numerous other texts that combine פסל + אלהים. In short, there exists only thin evidence that Deutero-Isaian idol polemic influenced Proto-Isaiah, and almost no evidence that sole divinity claims decisively influenced the final form of Proto-Isaiah.

Analogous Conceptions of YHWH's Supremacy

While there is little evidence that Deutero-Isaian monotheism or idol polemic directly influenced First Isaiah (or Third Isaiah for that matter), there are certain resonances between the ways that the two bodies of literature represent divine supremacy. I will address three features from this study that deserve reflection, by way of gesturing toward the need for a broader comparative theological study of divinity in Isaiah. By speaking of analogies, I am acknowledging the book's differing theological modes of expression that operate within the book's unrelenting insistence on YHWH's transcendent uniqueness.

First, both Proto- and Deutero-Isaiah engage in a rhetoric of reduction, which sometimes leads to a critique of idols. In First Isaiah, this occurs in *spatial* terms. First Isaiah frequently describes the humbling and abasement of humanity before YHWH using verbs such as *שפל* (14× in FI) and *שחח* (7× in FI). YHWH's campaign against all that is "raised high" results in everything being "made low" (*שפל*; 2:9, 11, 17). He brings down the proud (5:15), and lops off all tall trees (10:33), bringing down all the arrogant tyrants (13:11; cf. 25:11–12). All the אלילים are tossed *down* into caves and vanish (2:18, 20; cf. 31:7) because YHWH alone is exalted (2:9, 11, 17; 5:15). In addition to that spatial abasement, First Isaiah sometimes uses negation rhetoric. He draws attention to the reduction-to-nothing (אפס) of tyrants and powerful nations. The Moabites would cease, violence would end, and those who trample would disappear from the earth (16:4). Likewise, the ruthless would cease, and the evildoers be cut down (29:20). God's judgment on the nations would also bring an end to their nobles and princes (34:12). By contrast, only YHWH *alone* is exalted (*רום*, *שגב*, *נשא*).

Deutero-Isaiah deploys an analogous rhetorical strategy. He begins with an announcement that all high mountains will be "made low" (*שפל*; 40:4). But far more than spatial reduction, the prophet uses *rhetoric of negation*, with repeated use of words like אין and אפס. In other words, Deutero-Isaiah's rhetoric

---

16. Duhm, *Israels Propheten*, 285–91.

of reduction is less spatially construed. Before YHWH the nations are "as nothing" (כְּאַיִן) and "considered as less than nothing" (מֵאֶפֶס; 40:17). He reduces princes "to nothing" (לְאָיִן; 40:23), and renders Israel's enemies "as nothing" (כְּאַיִן 2×; 41:11–12). Idols are "as nothing" (מֵאָיִן, מֵאָפַע; 41:24). There was none other who spoke of the future (אַיִן, 5×; 41:26–28) such that the idols are all "nothing" (אֶפֶס; 41:29). We read then that apart from YHWH, "there is no savior" (מוֹשִׁיעַ . . . אֵין; 43:11–13). In these instances, the *language of negation* occurs within a broadscale rhetorical assault on all other would be agents, powers, and nations. The gods are just one of the powers that Deutero-Isaiah rhetorically levels. The effect is more comparative than ontological, and more totalizing than exclusively focused on the divine realm. From Isa 43–48, then, the rhetoric of negation pertains almost exclusively to YHWH. It shifts from all pretenders of power becoming "no one" toward the claim that there is "no one" but YHWH working on Israel's behalf.

Second, we could draw attention to the analogous ways that both First and Second Isaiah critique idol-*makers*. We observed how Isa 2 draws attention to the fact that the אֱלִילִים makers are frauds, just as the prophets were the frauds behind the אֱלִיל they espoused (Jer 14:14). In Isa 2:8 the prophet critiques the אֱלִילִים as "the works of their hands" and "that which their fingers had made." The prophet continues by referring to the אֱלִילִים as objects "which they made for themselves to worship" (v. 20). Their made-ness allowed the prophet to then pin all problems on the idol maker, an accusation that culminates in the call to "cease from humans, who only have breath in their nostrils" (v. 22). Isaiah 17:7–8 describes people turning away from the altars "that their fingers have made" toward the "Holy One of Israel."

Analogously, Deutero-Isaiah roundly mocks the idol-makers of Babylon (41:21–29; 44:9–20), along with those who bow down to them. MacDonald points out that such texts aim to draw a comparison between the Babylonian idols and Israel, and a contrast between YHWH and the Babylonians. Israel was uniquely fashioned by God but had become deaf, blind, and mute like the nations. YHWH had called them as his servant to "recognize YHWH's deeds and testify to them."[17] God had given Israel sight so that they could identify his works and not give credit to idols (48:5–11). Deutero-Isaiah contrasts not only YHWH and the Babylonian pantheon but also two competing sources of knowledge (prophecy vs. divination) and salvation (YHWH vs. Babylonian power). The prophet sought to awaken the people from their idol-like senselessness to see that only YHWH had declared the future and acted on their behalf.

Third, Proto- and Deutero-Isaiah highlight the sheer *folly* of idolatry, and the fact that YHWH is the exclusive source of wisdom. Scholars have long recognized the heavy use of wisdom language in Isaiah, but have not linked that

---

17. MacDonald, "Monotheism and Isaiah," 13.

theme to the prophet's use of אלילים. Given the term's relationship to "folly," this is surprising. I noted the heavy use of wisdom language in Isa 19, where YHWH announced that he would frustrate the counsel and wisdom of Egypt. Rather than driving the Egyptians from their idols and counselors, YHWH would drive Egypt toward them in order that they might reap the consequences of their foolishness. As Wildberger notes, YHWH's frustration of the nations' and Israel's "wisdom" sets the prophet's message in diametrical opposition "to the politics of making treaties, as advocated by the leaders in Jerusalem."[18] The prophet is obviously not opposed to wisdom as such, but rather to a specific political policy that mistrusts YHWH and leads to extreme hubris (e.g., 5:21). To highlight the folly of the nations' wisdom, and quite likely to undermine any trust in the nations, the prophet calls the idols אלילים, a term that epitomizes the folly of Egyptian, Assyrian, or any other nation's aid.

Deutero-Isaiah insists with some frequency that only YHWH can declare what is to come. As discussed, his exclusive grasp on the future distinguishes him categorically from other so-called deities (41:21–29). YHWH declared new things to the people in exile so the people could not claim their idols had told them (42:9; 44:7; 48:5). Moreover, only YHWH is able to *interpret* events, a claim that Goldingay observes is unique in the Old Testament.[19] In 41:22, for instance, "YHWH implicitly claims a unique ability to declare the significance of the events of history, and asks to be acknowledged as God on the basis of this ability."[20] Conversely, the idols cannot provide their devotees with any knowledge of the past, present, or future. In short, they were worthless, like the אלילים of Isa 1–39.

This theological comparison of Proto- and Deutero-Isaiah only scratches the surface of the kinds of issues that might lead us to distinguish or relate these two bodies of literature. We have not addressed the full range of issues impinging on how and whether one connects the two corpora. My study suggests that First Isaiah engages in its own mode of monotheizing that bears resemblances to other bodies of literature like the Deuteronomistic History or Deutero-Isaiah but is nevertheless distinct. It is distinct both in terms of its semantic choices, its spatial construal of divine supremacy, the rhetorical situations it addresses, and in terms of its general resistance to applying the term אלהים to other deities. First Isaiah opts instead for the dysphemistic אלילים, a mocking term designed to highlight the folly and ineptitude of idol veneration and its concomitant practices. Through such language "the gods" disappear from First Isaiah while simultaneously, the prophet exalts YHWH as "the sovereign" (האדון) in absolute terms. My hope is that this study advances the conversation about the varying shapes of monotheistic discourse, and about the remarkable theological contributions of the prophet we call First Isaiah.

18. Wildberger, *Isaiah 28–39*, 598.
19. Goldingay, *Message*, 136.
20. Ibid.

Appendixes

APPENDIX 1. Illicit Objects of Cultic Devotion

	אליל (זהב/כסף)	מעשה (ידים)	אלים	מסכה/מסכת (זהב)	פסל (זהב)	עצב	(זהב) מצבה (אבדה)	לא אלהים	תועבה	נסך	און	גזר	קבול	אוד	שקוץ	(actions) עשה* + היה*
First Isaiah																
2:6–22	4	1														2
10:10–11	2			1	1											
17:8		1	1	1												1
19:1–4	2															
21:9					1											
27:9		1	1	1												
30.:22				1		1										
31:7	2															1
37.:19		1					1									
Second Isaiah																
40:19–20								2								
41.:29									1							
42:1–17				1		1		1								
44:1–28								5		5						2
45:14–21								1		1	1					
46:1–7					1					1						1
48:5					1			1	1							
Third Isaiah																
57:12–13		1														
66:3														1	1	

APPENDIX 2. Spatial Rhetoric in Isaiah

	Rhetoric of Exaltation				Rhetoric of Abasement							
	רום (מרום)	נשא	קום	גאה (גאוה)	עלה	שפל	ירד	שחח	כלא	ירד	נפל	דמם
First Isaiah												
2:2–4			2		1							
2:6–22	5	3	2	3	3		4	3				
3:1–26			1	1							1	
5:14–16				2		2	1		1			
6:1	1		1									
7:1–6					2							
8:1–18					2						1	
9:1–21		1	1								1	
10:1–34	4		2	1		1	1		1	1	2	
11:12			1									
12:4		1										
13:1–22			1			1						
14:3–27		2			4	1			3	1		
15:1–5					1							
18:3			1									
21:9											2	
22:1–25	1				1							1
23:12–13		2										
24:1–23	3		1	1							2	
25:1–12	1					2	1					
26:1–21	2	1	2			2	1				1	
28:21			1									
29:3–4			1			1	1					
30:1–33	1	1		1	1						2	
31:1–9			1								1	
32:9–20	1						1			1		
33:5–12	2	1	1	1								
36:1–22					3							
37:1–38	2			1	2							
38:9–20										1		

	C1	C2	C3	C4	C5	C6	C7	C8	C9	C10	C11
Second Isaiah											
40:1–31	3			2	1	2		1			
42:10–17			1								
43.:17		1									
44.:23						1					
45.:23									1		
46:1–2									2		
47.:1										1	
49:3						1					
51:1–21		1	1								
52.:1–15	1		1	1	1						
55:1–13				2		1					
Third Isaiah											
57:1–21	2			2	1		1	3			
60:1–22			2			4					
61:1–11						3					
63:.6										1	
65:.12									1		

BIBLIOGRAPHY

Albertz, Rainer. *From the Beginnings to the End of the Monarchy.* Vol. 1 of *A History of Israelite Religion in the Old Testament Period.* Louisville: Westminster John Knox, 1994.

Albrektson, B. "The Divine Plan in History." Pages 68–97 in *History and the Gods: An Essay on the Idea of Historical Events as Divine Manifestations in the Ancient Near East and in Israel.* Coniectanea Biblica Old Testament 1. Lund: Gleerup, 1967.

Assmann, Jan. *Moses the Egyptian.* Cambridge: Harvard University Press, 1998.

Aster, Shawn Zelig. "The Image of Assyria in Isaiah 2:5–22: The Campaign Motif Reversed." *Journal of the American Oriental Society* 127 (2007): 249–78.

———. *Reflections of Empire in Isaiah 1–39: Responses to Assyrian Ideology.* Atlanta: SBL, 2017.

———. "Transmission of Neo-Assyrian Claims of Empire to Judah in the Late Eighth Century B.C.E." *Hebrew Union College Annual* 78 (2009): 1–44.

Bäckersten, Olaf. *Isaiah's Political Message: An Appraisal of His Alleged Social Critique.* FAT 2/29. Tübingen: Mohr Siebeck, 2008.

Balogh, Csaba. *The Stele of YHWH in Egypt: The Prophecies of Isaiah 18–20 Concerning Egypt and Kush.* Oudtestamentische Studiën 60. Leiden: Brill, 2011.

Barré, Michael L. "A Rhetorical-Critical Study of Isaiah 2:12–17." *Catholic Biblical Quarterly* 65 (2003): 522–34.

Barth, Hermann. *Die Jesaja-Worte in der Josiazeit: Israel und Assur als Thema einer produktiven Neuinterpretation der Jesajaüberlieferung.* Wissenschaftliche Monographien zum Alten und Neuen Testament 48. Neukirchen-Vluyn: Neukirchener Verlag, 1977.

Barton, George A. *The Religion of Israel.* New York: MacMillan, 1918.

Bauckham, Richard. *Jesus and the God of Israel: God Crucified and Other Studies on the New Testament's Christology of Divine Identity.* Grand Rapids: Eerdmans, 2008.

Becker, Uwe. *Jesaja, von der Botschaft zum Buch.* Forschungen zur Religion und Literatur des Alten und Neuen Testaments 178. Göttingen: Vandenhoeck & Ruprecht, 1997.

Berges, Ulrich. "Kingship and Servanthood in the Book of Isaiah." Pages 159–78 in *The Book of Isaiah: Enduring Questions Answered Anew; Essays Honoring Joseph*

Blenkinsopp and His Contributions to the Study of Isaiah. Edited by Richard J. Bautch and J. Todd Hibbard. Grand Rapids: Eerdmans, 2014.

Berges, Ulrich, and Willem A. M. Beuken. *Das Buch Jesaja: Eine Einführung*. Herders biblische Studienn 16. Göttingen: Vandenhoeck & Ruprecht, 2016.

Beuken, Willem A. M. *Jesaja 1–12*. Herders theologischer Kommentar zum Alten Testament. Freiburg: Herder, 2003.

Blenkinsopp, Joseph. "Fragments of Ancient Exegesis in an Isaian Poem (Jes 2,6–22)." *Zeitschrift für die Alttestamentliche Wissenscha* 93.1 (1981): 51–62.

———. *Isaiah 1–39*. Anchor Bible 19. New York: Doubleday, 2000.

Blum, Erhard. "Jesajas prophetisches Testament: Beobachtungen zu Jes 1–11 (Teil I)." *Zeitschrift für die Alttestamentliche Wissenscha* 108 (1996): 547–68.

Brekelmans, Christiaan H. W. "Deuteronomistic Influence in Isaiah 1–12." Pages 167–76 in *The Book of Isaiah—Le Livre D'Isaïe: Les Oracles et Leurs Relectures Unité et Complexité de L'Ouvrage*. Edited by Jacques Vermeylen. Leuven: Leuven University Press, 1989.

Brettler, Marc Zvi. *God Is King: Understanding an Israelite Metaphor*. Journal for the Study of the Old Testament Supplement 76. Sheffield: JSOT Press, 1989.

Brockelmann, Carl. *Grundriß der vergleichenden Grammatik der semitischen Sprachen*. 2 vols. Berlin: Reuther & Reichard, 1908–13.

Brueggemann, Walter. *Isaiah 1–39*. Westminster Bible Companion. Louisville: Westminster John Knox, 1998.

———. "Planned People/Planned Book?" Pages 19–37 in vol. 1 of *Writing and Reading the Scroll of Isaiah: Studies of an Interpretive Tradition*. Edited by Craig C. Broyes and Craig A. Evans. 2 vols. Leiden: Brill, 1997.

Carr, David M. *The Formation of the Hebrew Bible: A New Reconstruction*. New York: Oxford University Press, 2011.

Cazelles, Henri. "Qui aurait visé, à l'origine, Isaïe II 2–5?" *Vetus Testamentum* 30 (1980): 409–20.

Chan, Michael. "Rhetorical Reversal and Usurpation: Isaiah 10:5–34 and the Use of Neo-Assyrian Royal Idiom in the Construction of an Anti-Assyrian Theology." *Journal of Biblical Literature* 128 (2009): 717–33.

Childs, Brevard S. *Isaiah*. Old Testament Library. Louisville: Westminster John Knox, 2000.

Ciraolo, Leda Jean, and Jonathan Lee Seidel. *Magic and Divination in the Ancient World*. Leiden: Brill, 2002.

Clements, Ronald E. "Beyond Tradition-History: Deutero-Isaianic Developments of First Isaiah's Themes." *Journal for the Study of the Old Testament* 10 (1985): 95–113.

———. *Isaiah 1–39*. New Century Bible Commentary. Grand Rapids: Eerdmans, 1980.

Cohen, Chaim. "Neo-Assyrian Elements in the First Speech of the Biblical RAB-SAQE." *Israel Oriental Studies* 9 (1979): 32–48.

Cook, Paul M. *A Sign and a Wonder: The Redactional Formation of Isaiah 18–20*. Supplements to Vetus Testamentum 147. Leiden: Brill, 2011.

Couey, J. Blake. *Reading the Poetry of First Isaiah: The Most Perfect Model of the Prophetic Poetry*. Oxford: Oxford University Press, 2015.

Cryer, Frederick H. *Divination in Ancient Israel and Its Near Eastern Environment: A Socio-historical Investigation*. Journal for the Study of the Old Testament Supplement 142. Sheffield: JSOT Press, 1994.

Day, John. "Egyptian Wisdom Literature." Pages 17–29 in *Wisdom in Ancient Israel: Essays in Honour of J. A. Emerton*. Edited by John Day, Robert Gordon, and H. G. M. Williamson. Cambridge: Cambridge University Press, 1995.
Dick, Michael B., ed. *Born in Heaven, Made on Earth: The Making of the Cult Image in the Ancient Near East*. Winona Lake, IN: Eisenbrauns, 1999.
Duhm, Bernhard. *Das Buch Jesaia*. Göttingen: Vandenhoeck & Ruprecht, 1892.
———. *Israels Propheten*. Tübingen: Mohr Siebeck, 1916.
Dwyer, Philip. "Violence and Its Histories: Meanings, Methods, Problems." *History and Theory* 56.4 (2017): 7–22.
Fichtner, J. "Isaiah Among the Wise." Pages 428–38 in *Studies in Ancient Israelite Wisdom*. Edited by James Crenshaw. New York: KTAV, 1976.
———. "Jahwes Plan in der Botschaft des Jesaja." Pages 27–43 in *Gottes Weisheit: Gesammelte Studien zum Alten Testament*. Stuttgart: Calwer, 1965.
Fretheim, Terence E. "The Plagues as Ecological Signs of Historical Disaster." *Journal of Biblical Literature* 110 (1991): 385–96.
Friedländer, M., trans. *The Commentary of Ibn Ezra on Isaiah*. 2 vols. London: Trübner, 1873.
Goldingay, John. "The Compound Name in Isaiah 9:5(6)." *Catholic Biblical Quarterly* 61 (1999): 239–44.
———. *Isaiah 56–66*. International Critical Commentary. New York: Bloomsbury, 2014.
Goldingay, John, and David Payne. *Isaiah 40–55: A Critical and Exegetical Commentary*. Vol. 1. London: T&T Clark, 2006.
Gray, George B. *The Book of Isaiah, I–XXVII*. International Critical Commentary. Edinburgh: T&T Clark, 1912.
Gray, John. "The Kingship of God in the Prophets and Psalms." *Vetus Testamentum* 11 (1961): 1–29.
Greer, Jonathan S. *Dinner at Dan: Biblical and Archaeological Evidence for Sacred Feasts at Iron Age II Tel Dan and Their Significance*. Culture and History of the Ancient Near East 66. Boston: Brill, 2013.
Hallo, William H. "One God for Many: Philological Glosses on Monotheism." Pages 253–61 in *Mishneh Todah: Studies in Deuteronomy and Its Cultural Environment in Honor of Jeffrey H. Tigay*. Edited by Nili S. Fox, David A. Glatt-Gilad, and Michael J. Williams. Winona Lake, IN: Eisenbrauns, 2009.
Halpern, Baruch. "'Brisker Pipes Than Poetry': The Development of Israelite Monotheism." Pages 77–115 in *Judaic Perspectives on Ancient Israel*. Edited by Jacob Neusner, B. A. Levine, and E. S. Frerichs. Minneapolis: Fortress, 1987. Repr., B. A. Halpern, *From Gods to God: The Dynamics of Iron Age Cosmologies*. Edited by M. J. Adams. FAT 1/63. Tubingen: Mohr Siebeck, 2009, 13–56.
———. *From Gods to God: The Dynamics of Iron Age Cosmologies*. Edited by M. J. Adams. FAT 1/63. Tubingen: Mohr Siebeck, 2009.
———. "Jerusalem and the Lineages in the 7th Century BCE: Kinship and the Rise of Individual Moral Liability." Pages 11–107 in *Law and Ideology in Monarchic Israel*. Edited by B. Halpern and D. W. Hobson. Journal for the Study of the Old Testament Supplement 124. Sheffield: Sheffield Academic Press, 1991. Repr., B. A. Halpern, *From Gods to God: The Dynamics of Iron Age Cosmologies*. Edited by M. J. Adams. FAT 1/63. Tubingen: Mohr Siebeck, 2009, 339–424.
Hanson, Paul D. *A Political History of the Bible in America*. Louisville: Westminster John Knox, 2015.

Hayes, Katherine M. "A Spirit of Deep Sleep: Divinely Induced Delusion and Wisdom in Isaiah 1–39." *Catholic Biblical Quarterly* 74 (2012): 39–54.
Hays, Christopher B. *A Covenant with Death: Death in the Iron Age II and Its Rhetorical Uses in Proto-Isaiah*. Grand Rapids: Eerdmans, 2015.
———. *Death in the Iron Age II and in First Isaiah*. FAT 79. Tübingen: Mohr Siebeck, 2011.
———. "Enlil, Isaiah, and the Origins of the *'ĕlîlîm*: A Reassessment." *Zeitschrift für die Alttestamentliche Wissenschaft* 132 (2020): 224–35.
———. *The Origins of Isaiah 24–27: Josiah's Festival Scroll for the Fall of Assyria*. Cambridge: Cambridge University Press, 2019.
———. "Religio-Historical Approaches: Monotheism, Method, and Mortality." Pages 169–93 in *Method Matters: Essays on the Interpretation of the Hebrew Bible in Honor of David L. Petersen*. Atlanta: SBL, 2009.
———. "What Sort of Friends? A New Proposal Regarding (ם)רפאי and (ם)טפלי in Job 13,4." *Biblica* 90 (2009): 394–99.
Heim, Erin M. *Adoption in Galatians and Romans: Contemporary Metaphor Theories and the Pauline* Huiothesia *Metaphors*. Biblical Interpretation 153. Leiden: Brill, 2017.
Henderson, Joseph M. *Jeremiah Under the Shadow of Duhm: A Critique of the Use of Poetic Form as a Criterion of Authenticity*. London: T&T Clark, 2019.
Hodge, Carleton T. "Elilim." *Anthropological Linguistics* 25.2 (1983): 178–88.
Hoffmann, Hans Werner. *Die Intention der Verkündigung Jesajas*. Beiheft zur Zeitschrift für die alttestamentliche Wissenschaft 136. Berlin: de Gruyter, 1974.
Hoffner, Harry A., Jr. "Second Millennium Antecedents to the Hebrew *'ôb*." *Journal of Biblical Literature* 86 (1967): 385–401.
Jastrow, Morris, Jr. "The Element בשת in Hebrew Proper Names." *Journal of Biblical Literature* 13 (1894): 19–30.
Jensen, Joseph. "Yahweh's Plan in Isaiah and in the Rest of the Old Testament." *Catholic Biblical Quarterly* 48 (1986): 443–55.
Jeppesen, Knud. "The Cornerstone (Isa. 28: 16) in Deutero-Isaianic Rereading of the Message of Isaiah." *Studia Theologica* 38.1 (1984): 93–99.
Kaiser, Otto. *Isaiah 1–12*. Translated by John Bowden. Old Testament Library. London: SCM, 1983.
Kaufmann, Yehezkel. *The Religion of Israel*. Translated by Moshe Greenberg. Chicago: University of Chicago Press, 1960.
Keil, C. F., and F. Delitzsch. *Commentary on the Old Testament*. Vol. 7. Translated by Francis Bolton. Edinburgh: T&T Clark, 1892.
Killian, Rudolf. *Jesaja II. 13–39*. Neue Echter Bibel. Würzburg: Echter, 1994.
Kim, Kyun Chul Paul. "Little Highs, Little Lows: Tracing Key Themes in Isaiah." Pages 133–58 in *The Book of Isaiah: Enduring Questions Answered Anew; Essays Honoring Joseph Blenkinsopp and His Contribution to the Study of Isaiah*. Edited by Richard J. Bautch and J. Todd Hibbard. Grand Rapids: Eerdmans, 2014.
Kovecses, Zoltan. *Metaphor: A Practical Introduction*. Oxford: Oxford University Press, 2010.
Kratz, Reinhard G. *Kyros im Deuterojesaja-Buch: Redaktionsgeschichtliche Untersuchungen zu Entstehung und Theologie von Jes 40–55*. FAT 1. Tübingen: Mohr Siebeck, 1991.
Kutsko, John. *Between Heaven and Earth: Divine Presence and Absence in the Book of Ezekiel*. Biblical and Judaic Studies 7. Winona Lake, IN: Eisenbrauns, 2000.

Lee, Jongkyung. *A Redactional Study of the Book of Isaiah 13–23*. Oxford Theology and Religion Monographs. Oxford: Oxford University Press, 2018.

Levenson, Jon D. "The Universal Horizon of Biblical Particularism." Pages 143–69 in *Ethnicity and the Bible*. Edited by Mark G. Brett. Biblical Interpretation 19. Leiden: Brill, 1996.

Levine, Baruch A. "'Ah, Assyria! Rod of My Rage' (Isa. 10:15): Biblical Monotheism as Seen in an International, Political Perspective; A Prolegomenon." Pages 136–42 in *Eretz Israel* 27 (Tadmor Volume). Jerusalem: Israel Exploration Society, 2003. [Hebrew]

———. "Assyrian Ideology and Israelite Monotheism." *Iraq* 67 (2005): 411–27.

Luckenbill, D. D. *Ancient Records of Assyria and Babylonia.* 2 vols. Chicago: University of Chicago Press, 1927.

Lust, Johan. "The Divine Titles האדון and אדני in Proto-Isaiah and Ezekiel." Pages 131–49 in *Isaiah in Context*. Edited by Michaël N. van der Meer, Percy van Keulen, Wido van Peursen, and Bas Ter Haar Romeny. Leiden: Brill, 2010.

Lynch, Matthew J. "First Isaiah and the Disappearance of the Gods." Paper presented at the annual meeting of the Society of Biblical Literature, Baltimore, 23–26 November 2013.

———. "Mapping Monotheism: Modes of Monotheistic Rhetoric in the Hebrew Bible." *Vetus Testamentum* 64 (2014): 47–68.

———. *Monotheism and Institutions in the Book of Chronicles: Temple, Priesthood, and Kingship in Post-exilic Perspective*. FAT 2/64. Tübingen: Mohr Siebeck, 2014.

———. "Monotheism in Ancient Israel." Pages 340–48 in *Behind the Scenes of the Old Testament: Cultural, Social, and Historical Contexts*. Edited by Jonathan S. Greer, John W. Hilber, and John H. Walton. Grand Rapids: Baker Academic, 2018.

MacDonald, Nathan. *Deuteronomy and the Meaning of "Monotheism."* 2nd ed. FAT 2/1. Tübingen: Mohr Siebeck, 2012.

———. "Monotheism and Isaiah." Pages 43–61 in *Interpreting Isaiah: Issues and Approaches*. Edited by David G. Firth and H. G. M. Williamson. Nottingham: Apollos, 2009.

Machinist, Peter. "Assyria and Its Image in First Isaiah." *Journal of the American Oriental Society* 103 (1983): 719–37.

———. "Once More: Monotheism in Biblical Israel." *Journal of the Interdisciplinary Study of Monotheistic Religions* 1 (2005): 25–39.

Malamat, Abraham. "Campaigns to the Mediterranean by Iahdunlim and Other Early Mesopotamian Rulers." Pages 365–75 in *Studies in Honor of Benno Landsberger on His Seventy-Fifth Birthday, April 21 1965*. Edited by Hans Gustav Güterbock and Thorkild Jacobsen. Assyriological Studies 16. Chicago: University of Chicago Press, 1965.

Marti, D. Karl. *Das Buch Jesaja*. Tübingen: Mohr Siebeck, 1900.

Melugin, Roy F. *The Formation of Isaiah 40–55*. Beiheft zur Zeitschrift für die alttestamentliche Wissenschaft 141. Berlin: de Gruyter, 1976.

Mettinger, Tryggve N. D. *The Dethronement of Sabaoth: Studies in the* Shem *and* Kabod *Theologies*. Translated by Frederick H. Cryer. Coniectanea biblica Old Testament 18. Lund: Gleerup, 1982.

Metzger, Martin. *Königsthron und Gottesthron: Thronformen und Throndarstellungen in Ägypten und im Vorderen Orient im dritten und zweiten Jahrtausend vor Christus und deren Bedeutung für das Verständnis von Aussagen über den Thron im*

Alten Testament. 2 vols. Alter Orient und Altes Testament 15. Neukirchen-Vluyn: Neukirchener Verlag, 1985.

Mittmann, Siegfried "'Wehe! Assur, Stab meines Zorn" (Jes 10.5–9.13aß–15).'" Pages 111–33 in *Prophet und Prophetenbuch: Festschrift für Otto Kaiser zum 65 Geburtstag.* Edited by V. Fritz et al. Beiheft zur Zeitschrift für die alttestamentliche Wissenschaft 185. Berlin: de Gruyter, 1989.

Moberly, R. W. L. "How Appropriate Is 'Monotheism' as a Category for Biblical Interpretation?" Pages 216–234 in *Early Jewish and Christian Monotheism.* Edited by L. T. Stuckenbruck and W. E. Spronston North. Journal for the Study of the New Testament Supplement 263. Sheffield: Sheffield Academic, 2004.

———. "Whose Justice? Which Righteousness? The Interpretation of Isaiah V 16." *Vetus Testamentum* 51 (2001): 55–68.

Morenz, Siegfried. *Egyptian Religion.* Translated by Ann E. Keep. Ithaca: Cornell University Press, 1973.

Motyer, J. Alec. *The Prophecy of Isaiah: An Introduction and Commentary.* Downers Grove, IL: InterVarsity, 2015.

Odell, Margaret. "Did Ezekiel Condemn Idolatry? A Re-examination of the Nature and Function of the גלולים in the Book of Ezekiel." *Journal of Biblical Literature* (forthcoming).

O'Kane, Martin. "Wisdom Influence in First Isaiah." *Proceedings of the Irish Biblical Association* 14 (1991): 64–78.

Parpola, Simo. "The Assyrian Tree of Life: Tracing the Origins of Jewish Monotheism and Greek Philosophy." *Journal of Near Eastern Studies* 52 (1993): 161–208.

Paul, Shalom M. "Dysphemism." Page 550 in vol. 6 of *Encyclopedia Judaica.* 2nd ed. 22 vols. Farmington Hills, MI: Gale, 2006.

Petry, Sven. *Die Entgrenzung JHWHS: Monolatrie, Bilderverbot und Monotheismus im Deuteronomium, in Deuterojesaja und im Ezechielbuch.* FAT 2/27. Tübingen: Mohr Siebeck, 2007.

Podolsky, Baruch. "Notes on Hebrew Etymology." Pages 199–205 in *Past Links: Studies in the Languages and Cultures of the Ancient Near East.* Edited by Shlomo Israe'el, Itamar Singer, and Ran Zadok. Israel Oriental Studies 18. Winona Lake, IN: Eisenbrauns, 1988.

Pope, Marvin H. "Bible, Euphemism and Dysphemism in the." *ABD* 1:720–25.

———. "Euphemism and Dysphemism in the Bible." Pages 279–291 in *Probative Pontificating in Ugaritic and Biblical Literature: Collected Essays.* Edited by Mark S. Smith. Ugaritisch-Biblische Literatur 10. Münster: Ugarit-Verlag, 1994.

Preuss, Horst Dietrich. *Old Testament Theology.* Translated by Leo G. Perdue. Vol. 1. Louisville: Westminster John Knox, 1995.

Rad, Gerhard von. *Old Testament Theology: The Theology of Israel's Historical Traditions.* 2 vols. Translated by D. M. G. Stalker. Louisville: Westminster John Knox, 2001.

———. "The Origin of Mosaic Monotheism." Pages 128–38 in *God at Work in Israel.* Edited by Gerhard von Rad. Translated by J. H. Marks. Nashville: Abingdon, 1980.

Rendtorff, Rolf. "'*El* als israelitische Gottesbezeichnung: Mit einem Appendix: Beobachtungen zum Gebrauch von הָאֱלֹהִים." *Zeitschrift für die alttestamentliche Wissenschaft* 106 (1994): 4–21.

———. "Zur Komposition des Buches Jesaja." *Vetus Testamentum* 34 (1984): 295–320.

Roberts, J. J. M. *First Isaiah.* Hermeneia. Minneapolis: Fortress, 2015.

———. "Isaiah 2 and the Prophet's Message to the North." *Jewish Quarterly Review* 75 (1985): 290–308.

Satlow, Michael L. "Disappearing Categories: Using Categories in the Study of Religion." *Method and Theory in the Study of Religion* 17 (2005): 287–98.

Schipper, Bernd. "'The City by the Sea Will Be a Drying Place': Isaiah 19:1–25 in Light of Prophetic Texts from Ptolemaic Egypt." Pages 25–46 in *Monotheism in Late Prophetic and Early Apocalyptic Literature*. Edited by Nathan MacDonald and Ken Brown. Tübingen: Mohr Siebeck, 2014.

Schmid, H. H. *Wesen und Geschichte der Weisheit: Eine Untersuchung zur altorientalischen und israelitischen Weisheitsliteratur*. Beiheft zur Zeitschrift für die alttestamentliche Wissenschaft 101. Berlin: Töpelmann, 1966.

Schmidt, Brian B. *Israel's Beneficent Dead: Ancestor Cult and Necromancy in Ancient Israelite Religion and Tradition*. Winona Lake, IN: Eisenbrauns, 1994.

Schultz, Richard. "The King in the Book of Isaiah." Pages 141–65 in *The Lord's Anointed: Interpretation of Old Testament Messianic Texts*. Edited by Philip E. Satterthwaite, Richard S. Hess, and Gordon J. Wenham. Eugene, OR: Wipf & Stock, 1995.

Scullion, John J. "God." *ABD* 2:1043.

Seitz, Christopher R. "The Divine Council: Temporal Transition and New Prophecy in the Book of Isaiah." *Journal of Biblical Literature* 109 (1990): 229–47.

Simpson, William Kelly, ed. *The Literature of Ancient Egypt: An Anthology of Stories, Instructions, Stelae, Autobiographies, and Poetry*. New Haven: Yale University Press, 2003.

Smith, Jonathan Z. *Relating Religion: Essays in the Study of Religion*. Chicago: University of Chicago Press, 2004.

Smith, Mark S. "Monotheism and the Redefinition of Divinity in Ancient Israel." Pages 278–93 in *The Wiley Blackwell Companion to Ancient Israel*. Edited by Susan Niditch. Chichester: Wiley, 2016.

———. *The Origins of Biblical Monotheism: Israel's Polytheistic Background and the Ugaritic Texts*. New York: Oxford University Press, 2001.

———. "The Polemic of Biblical Monotheism: Outsider Context and Insider Referentiality in Second Isaiah." Pages 201–34 in *Religious Polemics in Context: Papers Presented to the Second International Conference of the Leider Institute for the Study of Religions (LISOR) Held at Leiden, 27–28 April 2000*. Edited by T. L. Hettema and A. van der Kooij. Assen: van Gorcum, 2004.

Sommer, Benjamin D. *The Bodies of God and the World of Ancient Israel*. New York: Cambridge University Press, 2009.

Steiner, Richard C. *Early Northwest Semitic Serpent Spells in the Pyramid Texts*. Harvard Semitic Studies 61. Winona Lake, IN: Eisenbrauns, 2011.

Strawn, Brent A. "The Etymology of בליעל Once Again: A Case of Tabooistic Deformation?" Forthcoming.

Stromberg, Jacob. *An Introduction to the Study of Isaiah*. T&T Clark Approaches to Biblical Studies. London: T&T Clark, 2011.

———. *Isaiah After Exile: The Author of Third Isaiah as Reader and Redactor of the Book*. Oxford: Oxford University Press, 2011.

Stuhlmueller, Carroll. "Deutero-Isaiah: Major Transitions in the Prophet's Theology and in Contemporary Scholarship." *Catholic Biblical Quarterly* 42 (1980): 1–29.

Sweeney, Marvin A. *Isaiah 1–4 and the Post-exilic Understanding of the Isaianic Tradition*. Beihefte zur Zeitschrift für die alttestamentliche Wissenschaft 171. Berlin: de Gruyter, 1988.

———. *Isaiah 1–39*. Forms of the Old Testament Literature 16. Grand Rapids: Eerdmans, 1996.

———. "Sargon's Threat Against Jerusalem in Isaiah 10,27–32." *Biblica* 75 (1994): 457–70.

Vermeylen, Jacques. *Du Prophète Isaïe à l'Apocalyptique: Isaïe, i–xxxv, miroir d'un demi-millénaire d'expérience religieuse en Israël*. Etudes Biblique 2. Paris: Gabalda, 1978.

Walker, Christopher, and Michael Dick. *The Induction of the Cult Image in Ancient Mesopotamia: The Mesopotamian* Mis Pî *Ritual*. State Archives of Assyria Literary Texts 1. Helsinki: University of Helsinki, 2001.

Watts, John D. *Isaiah 1–33*. Word Biblical Commentary 24. Waco, TX: Word, 1985.

Webb, Barry. "Zion in Transformation: A Literary Approach to Isaiah." Pages 65–84 in *The Bible in Three Dimensions: Essays in Celebration of Forty Years of Biblical Studies in the University of Sheffield*. Edited by David J. A. Clines, Stephen E. Fowl, and Stanley E. Porter. Journal for the Study of the Old Testament Supplement 87. Sheffield: JSOT Press, 1990.

Werner, Wolfgang. *Studien zur alttestamentlichen Vorstellung vom Plan Jahwes*. Beiheft zur Zeitschrift für die alttestamentliche Wissenschaft 173. Berlin: de Gruyter, 1988.

Whedbee, J. William. *Isaiah and Wisdom*. Nashville: Abingdon, 1971.

Wieringen, Archibald L. H. M. van. "Isaiah 24:21–25:12: A Communicative Analysis." Pages 77–97 in *Formation and Intertextuality in Isaiah 24–27*. Edited by J. Todd Hibbard and Hyun Chul Paul Kim. Society of Biblical Literature Ancient Israel and Its Literature 17. Atlanta: SBL, 2013.

Wildberger, Hans. *Isiaah 1–12*. Translated by Thomas H. Trapp. Minneapolis: Fortress, 1991.

———. *Isaiah 13–37*. Translated by Thomas H. Trapp. Minneapolis: Fortress, 1997.

———. *Isaiah 38–39*. Translated by Thomas H. Trapp. Minneapolis: Fortress, 2002.

———. "Jesajas Verständnis der Geschichte." Pages 83–117 in *Congress Volume: Bonn, 1962*. Vetus Testamentum Supplement 9. Leiden: Brill, 1962.

Williamson, H. G. M. *The Book Called Isaiah: Deutero-Isaiah's Role in Composition and Redaction*. Oxford: Clarendon, 1994.

———. *A Critical and Exegetical Commentary on Isaiah 1–27*. 2 vols. International Critical Commentary 20/1. London: T&T Clark, 2006.

———. "Idols in Isaiah in the Light of Isaiah 10:10–11." Pages 17–28 in *New Perspectives on Old Testament Prophecy and History: Essays in Honour of Hans M. Barstad*. Edited by Rannfrid I. Thelle, Terje Stordalen, and Mervyn E. J. Richardson. Vetus Testamentum Supplement 168. Leiden: Brill, 2015.

———. *Isaiah 1–5*. Vol. 1 of *A Critical and Exegetical Commentary on Isaiah 1–27*. International Critical Commentary. London: T&T Clark, 2006.

———. "A Productive Textual Error in Isaiah 2:18–19." Pages 377–88 in *Essays on Ancient Israel in Its Near Eastern Context: A Tribute to Nadav Na'aman*. Edited by Y. Amit, Ehud Ben Zvi, Israel Finkelstein, and Oded Lipschits. Winona Lake, IN: Eisenbrauns 2006.

Wilson, Lindsay. "Wisdom in Isaiah." Pages 145–67 in *Interpreting Isaiah: Issues and Approaches*. Edited by David G. Firth and H. G. M. Williamson. Downers Grove, IL: IVP Academic, 2009.

Wilson, Robert. *Prophecy and Society in Ancient Israel.* Philadelphia: Fortress, 1980.

Wolff, Hans Walter. "Jahwe und die Götter in der alttestamentlichen Prophetie." *Evangelische Theologie* 29 (1969): 397–416.

INDEX OF SUBJECTS

abasement, rhetoric of   1, 16–18, 19, 27–30, 31–33, 35–36, 38–42, 46, 48, 71–75, 104, 108–9
Assyria/Assyrian(s)   xiv, 2–11, 16–18, 21–23, 30, 33, 44–46, 57, 61–63, 65–75, 82, 84–85, 90, 96, 99, 101, 106
Deuteronomistic   xiv, 6, 17, 24, 50, 52–55, 80, 98, 106
dysphemism(s)   1, 23–26
Egypt/Egyptian(s)   13, 18, 22, 33, 43–45, 47, 57, 76–83, 85, 87–92, 96–97, 99, 102, 105
exaltation, rhetoric of   1, 7–8, 15–17, 20, 27–34, 35–41, 46–48, 50–51, 55, 59–60, 61–67, 71, 73, 75, 98, 100, 104, 106, 108–9
folly/foolishness   18, 23–24, 26, 44, 46–48, 76, 79, 81–83, 85–92, 96–99, 105–6
gods   xiv, 1, 3–4, 6, 8–10, 18, 19, 21–27, 35, 36, 42–44, 46–49, 51–54, 57–59, 61, 63–68, 70, 75–79, 81, 88–89, 91–93, 95–96, 98–99, 101, 103, 105–6
idols/idolatry   xiii–xiv, 1, 4, 15, 18, 20–26, 32, 36–37, 41–50, 53–60, 61–67, 77–82, 89, 91, 93, 95–96, 98–106
idols in Isaiah, terms for   107–8
images   18, 25–26, 29, 32, 47–49, 51, 54, 56–57, 61, 63, 65, 67, 71, 89, 91, 98–100, 103
metaphor, spatial   xiii, 7, 16–17, 27–34, 38, 98
monotheism, definitions of   12–15
monotheism and First Isaiah   xiii–xiv, 1, 6, 7–12, 15–17, 27, 35, 52, 55, 59, 69, 98–99, 104–6
monotheism and Second Isaiah   xiii–xiv, 1, 35, 52, 99–106
plans   4, 46, 62–63, 76, 81, 83–89, 92, 97, 99
polemic   9, 41, 50–51, 80, 98, 103–4
rhetoric   xiii–xiv, 1–2, 7–8, 10–18, 19, 21, 23–24, 27–28, 30–31, 34, 36–38, 52, 56, 58–59, 66–67, 70–71, 73–75, 97, 98–102, 104–6
sovereign, (the)   8, 16–17, 29, 67–75, 78, 88, 98–99, 106
wisdom   28, 76–79, 81–83, 85–92, 96–97, 105–6

INDEX OF AUTHORS

Albertz, R.   4, 5
Aster, S.   9, 70
Barré, M. L.   39
Barth, H.   62
Barton, G.   2, 3
Becker, U.   66, 67
Berges, U.   73, 74
Blenkinsopp, J.   36, 37, 43, 50, 65, 66
Brekelmans, C.   51
Brueggemann, W.   86
Cazelles, H.   50
Chan, M.   70, 71
Childs, B.   36, 37, 66, 71, 72
Clay, A. T.   21
Cook, P.   94
Goldingay, J.   25, 45, 101, 106
Gray, G.   3
Halpern, B.   5, 8
Hayes, K.   90
Hays, C. B.   21, 22, 32
Heim, E. M.   33
Hodge, C.   20
Jensen, J.   87
Kaiser, O.   52
Kim, H. C. P.   31

Kövecses, Z.   28
Kutsko, J.   15, 26, 54, 55
Levine, B.   7, 8, 10, 17
Lust, J.   67, 68
MacDonald, N.   5, 11, 12, 50, 74, 101, 105
Machinist, P.   8, 70
Petry, S.   15
Podolsky, B.   21
Pope, M.   20, 24
Preuss, H.   72
Rad, G. von   3, 4, 11, 12
Roberts, J. J. M.   39, 42, 44, 58
Schmid, H. H.   83
Scullion, J.   1
Smith, J. Z.   12, 13
Smith, M. S.   5
Strawn, B. A.   24, 28
Stromberg, J.   84
Webb, B.   103
Werner, W.   86, 87
Wildberger, H.   44, 57, 72, 86, 87, 106
Williamson, H. G. M.   15–16, 20, 51, 52, 63, 64, 102

INDEX OF SCRIPTURE

Exodus
  7:11   80–81
  12:12   78
  15:13   81
  20:23   49, 54–55
  34   49

Leviticus
  11:19   47
  19:4   48–49, 102
  26:1   48–49, 102

Deuteronomy
  4:35   69
  5:8   49
  7:25   54
  12:3   103
  14:18   47
  18   89, 94–95
  27:15   52
  32:16   25

Joshua
  3:11–13   69

2 Samuel
  2:8   24
  4:4   24
  11:21   24

1 Kings
  4:29   28
  12:31   25

2 Kings
  18:33–34   65
  19:18   52
  21:6   80
  23:24   80

Isaiah
  1:2   32
  1:3   88
  1:24   69, 73
  2   16–17, 31
  2:1–5   33, 35, 38
  2:5   48, 58
  2:5–22   32
  2:6–8   37, 41–43
  2:6–22   17, 35–60
  2:7–8   91–92
  2:8   46–50, 52–53, 55–56, 105
  2:9–11   40
  2:11   17, 28–30, 35
  2:12   28–30
  2:12–13   71
  2:12–17   32–34, 37, 38–41
  2:16   32
  2:17   17, 28–29, 35, 40, 46
  2:18   46–50
  2:19–21   34, 35, 41
  2:20   46–50, 54, 56, 91
  3:1   69
  3:2–3   89
  3:5   79
  3:8   29
  5:15–16   16, 31, 35, 40
  5:21   88
  6   3, 16, 33
  6:1   29, 35
  6:4   79
  6:5   69, 73
  7   83–84
  7:14   45
  7:18   24
  8   83–84
  8:12–13   36
  8:16–18   92–93
  8:19   18
  8:19–21   92–97
  8:23   80
  9:5   45
  10:5–9   63
  10:5–15   18
  10:5–19   61–75
  10:8–11   64–67
  10:10   21–22
  10:10–11   62–65
  10:13   88
  10:16   67, 69
  10:28–32   71
  10:33–34   29, 32, 67, 69–71
  12:4   29
  14:3–27   33
  14:11–19   73–74
  14:15   29

Isaiah (cont.)
  14:24–27   84
  17:7–8   36, 50, 55–56, 57–58, 105
  19   76–97, 105
  19:1   89
  19:1–4   18, 69, 77–81, 92
  19:3   22, 79–80, 89, 92–97
  19:4   80–81, 88
  19:11   81, 87
  19:11–15   81–83, 89, 96
  19:12   85, 88, 92
  19:14   82, 90
  19:15   82
  19:16–25   82
  19:17   81, 85, 89, 92
  20:1–6   82, 96–97
  21:9   103
  22:8–11   45
  23:1–14   85, 88
  24:20   29
  24:21   74
  25:1–5   87
  26:13   68
  29:4   93
  29:10   90
  29:14   89–90
  29:15   90
  29:23   53
  30:1–2   90–91, 97
  30:6   45
  30:19–20   36
  30:22   91
  30:25   29
  30:33   29
  31:1–3   43–46, 90–91, 97
  31:6–7   36, 44, 54, 56, 91
  31:8   45
  32:1–8   85
  32:19   31
  33:5   29, 31
  36–39   17
  36:18–20   18, 64–67
  37:12–13   65
  37:16   72
  37:19   52
  37:26   84
  40   31, 104
  40–55   99–106
  41:22   106
  44:8   69
  44:9–20   51
  45:5   3, 68
  45:18   3
  45:21   68
  45:22   3
  50:2   81
  60:21   53
  64:3   101–2

Jeremiah
  3:24   24
  14:14   19–20, 89, 105
  51:8   104

Ezekiel
  20:32   54

Hosea
  4:15   24
  5:8   24
  10:5   24

Micah
  2:5   58

Zechariah
  4:14   69
  6:5   69
  14:14   21

Psalms
  8:4   47, 53
  29   41
  96:5   102
  97:5   69
  97:7   102
  115:4   53
  135:15   53
  144   48

Job
  13:4   19, 21

Song of Songs
  7:2   53

Lamentations
  4:2   53

www.ingramcontent.com/pod-product-compliance
Lightning Source LLC
Chambersburg PA
CBHW030526080526
44586CB00011B/338